Introduction

You walk into a room.

- People look at you with appreciation. They are glad you are here.

- They listen to each word you say.

- You listen to them and incorporate their ideas into your next sentences.

- You offer a story or example. You smile and laugh easily.

- You have become The Person People Pay Attention To.

This will be you.

Executive Speaking in a Weekend

Step by Step Templates for Commanding Respect and Creating Results

Reesa Woolf, PhD

PBP
Business Publications
Press

Printed in the United States of America

Library of Congress Cataloging-In-Publication

Woolf, Reesa.

    Executive Speaking in a Weekend: Steps and Templates for Commanding Respect and Creating Results/Reesa Woolf. – 1st.ed. – Business Publications Press
    p. ; cm.

    ISBN: 978-1-935598-75-6
    Summary: The competent person who speaks well has an unlimited career. Reesa Woolf, PhD gives you best practices of proven Executive Speaking Training.

    Public Speaking—United States. 2. Business—United States. 3. Professional Growth—United States. I. Title.

Executive Speaking in a Weekend is available at special quantity discounts for sales promotions, premiums, fund-raising or educational use. Special books and book excerpts can be created to customize for your organization.

Inquiries: www.SpeakLikeAnExecutive.com

Table of Contents

Praise for Reesa Woolf, PhD

"Reesa is a tremendous presenter, a caring teacher and a subject matter expert extraordinaire." **Robert Astle, Patron Spirits**

"Reesa is a trainer's trainer. Her ability to connect and help people communicate is effectively second to none." **Adam Ayers, Siemens**

"Reesa Woolf, PhD, gives us the template and tools of an engaging speaker that will serve in your career and personal life forever." **Adam Lech, Dassault Falcon Jet**

"Reesa Woolf, PhD, is a master at producing people at their best. Finally, her dependable guidelines are available in this remarkable book. Read this book as if your career depends on it." **Jandry Bernal, PepsiCo**

"Executive Speaking in a Weekend is the go-to practical reference for becoming a great speaker. **David Rector, Nielsen Ratings International**

Reesa Woolf counters myths and fears to make great speaking available to everyone." **Hilda Canas, Roche Pharmaceuticals**

Our 8th year! Dr. Woolf conducts the seminar professionally and makes it fun and personal. **Susan Storms, Director, John D. Rockefeller International House, NYC**

"Thank you so much, Reesa. Those days with you will be life changing for me, in whatever the language! Keep doing the good job!" **Thony (Tony) Moise, Director, Sofihdes**

"Reesa, I said it multiple times during the seminar, but it is worth repeating, Thank you. Taking your workshop was a fantastic experience.

I've already used pieces learned several times today. This morning when my neighbor asked how my run went, I summed it up very succinctly using the outline from the mapping exercise. I even remembered a solid close! This evening, I spoke in front of my town's planning committee. I didn't really need to speak, but it was good to reinforce what others were saying – and once again, I said it clearly and strongly. More importantly, I actually wanted to get up there and talk. It's fun!

Thanks again for the fantastic growth experience." **Jane Rein**

"I immediately received compliments from peers and bosses when I used your simple techniques." **Robin Pulverenti, DCMA - Defense Contract Management Agency**

"Reesa is a jewel and a valuable resource for executive development. Her individual training is excellent." **Jerry Li, McKinsey**

CHAPTER 1

Confident Speaking

**"Would you mind addressing the
Annual Meeting in 10 minutes?"**

Communication - Definition

**"Communication means transferring your ideas to other
people. The amount of information transferred
is the measure of your success."**

> ### TIP
> Confident speakers know that communication does not mean "just getting through my notes."

You are Competing With One Thing Each Time you Speak

You are competing with each listener's own chattering voice inside of their heads - the never-ending commentary called "self-talk." Their self-talk is still speaking to them *while you speak to them.*

How to Attract and Keep Listeners' Attention

In *Executive Speaking in a Weekend,* you will learn many techniques to capture listeners' interest when you begin speaking, and how to recapture attention again and again throughout your talk, as their mind's wander. Listeners will stay with you until you finish.

You will know how to...

- Write compelling messages.
- Use the tone and volume of your voice (Voice Variety) to highlight your most important ideas.
- Incorporate "Supports" to increase understanding and retention. Some Supports are "imagine," analogies, examples, quotations, and "benefits to them."

Listeners have only Two Rules

Listener Rule #1: Don't Waste my Time
Listener Rule #2: End on Time

Listener Rule #1: Don't Waste my Time

People decide in the first seconds of each of your talks if it is worth listening to you.

To appear confident and authoritative as you begin, rehearse your first sentences, known as the Opener, *aloud*. Aim to use the delivery (voice tone, volume, eye contact and gestures) you will use in your real talk.

Rehearse the last sentences, the Close, to end smoothly and with strength.

> **TIP**
> When you do not have time to rehearse the whole talk, at least practice the Opener and Close aloud.

How to Not Waste Their Time

© Randy Glasbergen. www.glasbergen.com

"Good afternoon. I'm not prepared, I'm filling in for someone else. I'm in the early stages of dementia, I don't have anything new to say and I'm slightly hung over, but I hope you enjoy this."

- Create User-friendly notes to keep on track, a minimum outline with only topic cues and important words on it. This format encourages you to speak conversationally to connect with people and not read your notes at them.
- Memorize only the Opener and Close.
- Do not read PowerPoint screens to them. Why? Because when you show a screen, the listeners will automatically read your material. Reading it to them after that would waste their time. Instead, refer to a bullet and elaborate on it.

- Speak Concisely: If you *know* you talk too much or frequently digress from a topic, eliminate introductory material and details. Give only what listeners need to know. Ask a colleague who speaks succinctly to listen to your rehearsal and make editing suggestions. If you do this eight times, you will know how to stay focused.

What To Do When you Lose Their Attention

- Don't ignore it: If you disregard the audience's obvious cues that they are bored and continue giving the talk you have prepared, the listeners will not only resent having their time wasted, they will also know you haven't been paying attention to them.
- To win them back, stop talking and adjust the content based on their feedback. Say, "What questions do you have?" or "I don't think I'm giving you the information you want. Am I being too technical or too basic? Please let me know what you'd prefer."

  If no one answers, suggest that the audience break into small groups for a minute to come up with suggestions on what they would like to hear.
- Or you can initiate a group question and answer session. They will respect you for addressing their issues.

Listener Rule #2: End on Time

- Listeners appreciate when you honor the schedule, especially before lunch or the end of the day. End on time even if others in your organization do not.

  Example: A pre-lunch speaker at a convention had the listeners enthralled. When he spoke longer than his allotted time and made them late for their meal, people got restless and resented him. Irrational reaction, but true.

- Exception - It is a different issue when the boss makes you late with a question. Make the boss happy.

CHAPTER 2

How to Correct a Mistake

Confident Speakers Make Mistakes

- You *will* make mistakes when you speak. Notice that experienced speakers make errors each time they speak, such as beginning a word and changing it to a different word or going back to add something they had forgotten.
- In the workplace, some things must be done perfectly and some things can never be done perfectly.
  - ○ Pretend to draw a line vertically down the center of a piece of paper. Label the left column *Must be Perfect* and the right side *Can Never Be Perfect*.
  - ○ Parts of your job that must be done perfectly belong in the left column. *Speaking* is on the right side of the page, the *Can Never Be Perfect* side.

What to do with a Mistake

Correct Mistakes and Keep Speaking

Experienced speakers expect mistakes, fix them and do not mention the mistake again. They know that listeners will forget about the mistake and are only concerned with receiving accurate information.

Notice how accomplished speakers react when they make a mistake. Their behavior is similar to the advice we might say to a child in a concert, "Honey, if you make a mistake, keep playing."

Even if a misstep bothers them, they don't show it. They keep acting as though they feel confident.

Use "Saves"

Memorize a few lines to say when you make mistakes such as,

- "What I meant to say was _____."
- "My mistake. It is _____."
- "Let me change that. The number is..."
- "I want to add one more thing to that section..."
- Joke: "I've never made a mistake before, but this could be the first time..."

After you correct the mistake, *continue speaking as if nothing unusual has happened.*

When *you act* as though the error was just a small oversight, listeners will not be distracted.

What Not to Do

Errors that People Make with Mistakes

- Their faces look shocked.
- They say things like, "I can't believe I said that, I am so sorry, I really did prepare" or similar overly-apologetic statements.
- As a result, the listeners begin to feel bad because the emotions of the speaker are contagious.

© Randy Glasbergen / glasbergen.com

"We hardly noticed the mistake, but the horrified look on his face is burned in my memory forever."

Preparation

- When you make errors in rehearsal, do not stop or start over! Correct mistakes in rehearsal just as you will "save" them in the real talk.
- When you forget an essential word or an idea while practicing, add it to your notes.
- When you overlook something written on your notes, highlight it to make be easier to see and remember to say in the real talk.

TIP

Don't increase your anxiety by thinking, "I hope I don't make any mistakes." Delete that thought. Since *you will make mistakes,* aiming for speaking perfection is an absurd goal.

CHAPTER 3

Look Confident, Even When You Don't Feel It

Eyes, Face, Hands, Feet & Posture

Have you seen smart people, with well-written talks, ruin their presentations with mediocre delivery?

To appear confident and help your listeners receive more of what you say, control and *purposely* communicate with your eyes, face, hands, feet and posture.

> ### TIP
> Confident Speakers are careful to do, and not do, certain things with their body language when speaking to anyone.

The Secret to Great Body Language is Congruence

- If your words say one thing, but your face, eyes, hands, feet or posture indicate a different meaning, listeners will believe the message communicated by your body language 100% of the time. *Always*.
- To appear to be a charismatic speaker, become skilled at making your body language synchronize with your message.
- You may feel like an actor – yes, you are acting like your most appealing self, even when you don't feel it inside. This serves both your message and the listeners.

The Techniques Confident Speakers use with Body Language

Eyes

In the U.S., if you don't make Eye Contact, people might think you are lying.

- Looking people in the eye shows that you want them to hear and understand your message.
- Eye contact helps you to appear confident.
- Do not look so deeply into any person's eyes that you get distracted from your notes and your talk.
- When you speak in different countries and different cultures, use the eye contact they use.

WATCH VIDEO ON EYES

WWW.EXECUTIVESPEAKINGINAWEEKEND.COM/EYES

"But I dislike looking directly at people's eyes."

- When you look at the top of the nose, the bridge of the nose, it will appear that you are looking directly at the person. This could minimize uncomfortable feelings while looking at intimidating people.
- An alternative is to imagine that your listeners have blurred faces, as on some television news stories. Still look where the eyes are since it is imperative to appear as if you are making eye contact.

"How should I look around the room?"

Whether you are looking at four people or four hundred, divide the group into quadrants. Look at people in one area for about five seconds. Then look at people in another part for five seconds. Then another; repeat.

Mistakes made with Eyes

When you are nervous, you may look at one person, or one quadrant, or one side of the room, or the notes, or above people's heads. This tells the group you are nervous. You will seem confident by using the four quadrant method.

> **TIP**
>
> Do not look at the quadrants in the same order each time - mix it up or people will notice the technique.

"I get nervous speaking to a large group."

- What number of people can you speak to without getting nervous? Two? Four? Six? In a large group, find that number of people in each quadrant. Look at them and make your mind block out everyone else. Speak only to your small group in your usual conversational way.

- The entire room will hear more of what you say because they see you are "just explaining things to us and helping us to learn."

- How do you get used to using the four quadrants? Rehearse in or imagine yourself in the room where you will actually be speaking - sit in the chair you might use and visualize your listeners watching you. Actually move your head and eyes to connect with one area for about five seconds before moving on.

- You can rehearse this in your own home - draw faces on paper and paste them on chairs around a table.

Referring to Notes

1. Break eye contact to look at notes and capture the next idea. Be silent when you do this since you can't be heard well if you speak while looking down.

2. Look up from notes, make eye contact and begin speaking again.

A good time to glance at notes is right after you reveal a new visual. The audience will be busy reading the new screen or page.

When should you *not* look at Notes?

Confident speakers seize attention with this important technique: rehearse the Opener and Close so you can deliver both with 100% eye contact. Keep them brief to be easily remembered without having to glance at notes.

Speaking to One Person

Look at that person's face (or the bridge of the nose) for about 80% of the conversation. The rest of the time you will be consulting notes or gazing away to remember and generate ideas (It is a human trait to "look away" as we think).

Face

Facial Movement is Good

The expressions of confident speakers reflect their messages; this adds believability. They look thoughtful when discussing a serious issue and happy while discussing light-hearted topics and good news.

WATCH VIDEO ON FACE

WWW.EXECUTIVESPEAKINGINAWEEKEND.COM/FACE

Your Smile is a Most Important Gesture!

It is natural to smile when saying or thinking about something good.

- Your smile indicates that you have a warm personality. Therefore, smile as you greet people.
- If your news is good, establish rapport by smiling even before you speak.
- Remind yourself to smile at certain points by placing a symbol such as a star, in color, on your notes.

"How big should I smile?"

Do not use a big fake smile. A small grin will work.

Improving Facial Gestures

If you want to increase your use of appropriate facial gestures, a good exercise is to look in the mirror at home as you speak on the phone. Consciously make your face congruent with what you say.

Establish Rapport More Quickly

People in rapport naturally do something called "mirroring." They unconsciously imitate other's communication patterns.

You can help people feel more comfortable with you by coordinating your face to what *they* say. Purposely look interested, surprised, sad, glad, etc. (whatever their feelings indicate).

Hands

Hand Movements to Avoid

- Fidgeting. Playing with your ring as you speak says to others, "I'm nervous." Of course, you *are nervous* but you don't want to alert the audience.
- Do not point at people with pens, forks, knives, chopsticks or an index finger. Gesture with your palm facing up.
- Break the habit of touching your hair or clothes.
- Be mindful: As soon as you notice you are fidgeting... stop. Practice in front of a mirror or video yourself to raise your awareness of distracting behaviors.

WATCH VIDEO ON HANDS

WWW.EXECUTIVESPEAKINGINAWEEKEND.COM/HANDS

Hands in Pockets

- Most people keep their hands in their pockets because they don't know what to do with them.
- You will move your hands when they are in your pockets. People will look at that part of your body. It is preferable to have them look at your face.

The Best use of Hands and Gestures

Notice your hands as you speak with friends; you move them naturally, often in synch with your content. Imitate that behavior as you give a talk. Moving your hands appropriately makes you appear enthused and energetic.

Suggestions

- Keep hands above the waist.
- In rehearsal, exaggerate acting out real words such as, "work together" (fingers laced together), "stop" (palm facing the person), "A to Z" (hand gesture right to left), "one, two, three" (hold fingers up and still as you indicate the number), "this group or that" (a hand motioning to each side), etc.
- Select the gestures you actually want to use. On your notes, draw a color picture of hands making that movement.
- Eliminate repetitious movements because they distract listeners. And do not act out every word.
- When to minimize or *not* use gestures? Study and reflect your audience's style. If the group is reserved or if you are speaking in a country where gestures would make you look ridiculous, obviously make the effort to match your listeners.

At a lectern

Do not hold the sides of the lectern. Either use no gestures or include those that best illustrate your message.

Some people keep one hand on their printed notes to keep track of their place.

Feet

- Stand in one place with weight equal on both feet. Have feet as far apart as your shoulders. Do not move from the waist down (your voice, face and arms should be animated).
- When you want to move, take a couple of steps and replant your feet.
- Do not: pace, take a small step as you begin a new topic, lean on one leg, bounce on your heels, lift up your toes or bend your knees.
- Rehearse in front of a mirror if you are unaware of what your feet do. To help yourself stand still, imagine that your feet are glued to the floor.
- Plan your movements. Perhaps just before saying something significant, take some intentional steps.
- Draw movement reminders on your notes - draw simple feet or make up a symbol and place it above or between ideas. Use a color different than your notes.
- Keep feet still when behind a lectern - the audience can see you pace or bounce.

Posture

- Standing fully upright makes you appear powerful. Your body should be vertical and not leaning on a diagonal.

WATCH VIDEO ON POSTURE

WWW.EXECUTIVESPEAKINGINAWEEKEND.COM/POSTURE

- Instead of standing at "military rest" with shoulders pulled way back, simply push your head and spine toward the ceiling.
- Avoid wiggling your midsection sideways or forward and back.

Clothing

Copyright 2002 by Randy Glasbergen.   www.glasbergen.com

"Fear of public speaking is quite common.
If dressing up as Speaker Man makes you
feel more confident, then so be it."

- Be strategic: if you are ambitious, dress like the bosses so it is easy for them to envision you in the next higher position. Sometimes it is appropriate to dress like the listeners.

- The latest fashion is not important unless you are in an industry that values it.

- Keep a jacket at work as an option to wear in impromptu meetings.

- Eyeglasses are a way to appear up-to-date. Trust the taste of the people at the optometrist's office when choosing frames. Get non-glare lenses with no visible bifocal lines. If you need reading glasses but have good far-vision, consider bifocals with a clear top and reading glasses on the bottom - a better choice than glasses perched on the middle of your nose, or putting on and removing glasses throughout your talk.

- Do not wear distracting ties, clothing, jewelry or shoes, especially with new listeners. If a type of clothing, such as a tie, is your "signature," explain it to avoid distraction.

- Scents: Wear none. No exceptions.

- Be polished. Keep your shoes shined and heels in good repair. Tidy nails are all filed to the same length. Nail polish should be on or off (not semi-rubbed off). Follow the lead of upper management about having designs painted on nails.

- Hair, men and women - Ask your haircutter for suggestions on looking the best you can. Occasionally try a new salon.

- Women's makeup - Allow a professional to update your makeup every three years. Trust someone who does not look like a clown.

CHAPTER 4

Sound Confident When You Don't Feel It

TIP

Please do not skip this chapter. It is an equally important part of capturing and holding attention.

Your Voice

Excellent speakers use their voices to punctuate important ideas and sound truthful and authentic.

Use best practices when speaking will improve listener comprehension. You may have to adjust your habitual ways of speaking.

WATCH VIDEO ON VOICE

WWW.EXECUTIVESPEAKINGINAWEEKEND.COM/VOICE

"But I'm comfortable speaking the way I do!"

It is fine to speak the way that is most comfortable for you... at home.

To successfully transfer the most information, use the speaking volume and rate of speed that your listeners prefer, even if it is not how you typically speak.

Best Speaking Practices

Speak Loud Enough

If you have been asked in this past year to speak louder, you are probably speaking too softly.

Check with others, especially a boss, to make sure you speak at the volume that is expected by the listeners. Make sure your voice can be easily heard by the person sitting farthest away.

WATCH VIDEO ON LOUD ENOUGH

WWW.EXECUTIVESPEAKINGINAWEEKEND.COM/LOUDENOUGH

When you speak too quietly, your listeners have to work to hear you - and they won't work at it for long. Their own self-talk will take their attention away from you.

Also, speaking too quietly allows for louder colleagues to interrupt and completely pull the audience's attention away from you.

What to do

Ask a friend to coach you to speak using a level of loudness that is appropriate to your workplace. Feedback helps because you may inaccurately think you are already loud enough. When you increase the volume, you may sense that you are yelling even when you really are not. Although you may not ever be comfortable speaking this way, trust your friend's opinion and use your new volume in each meeting, on each telephone call and teleconference.

When you have an important telephone call and are concerned that your louder voice may disturb co-workers, make the call from the conference room.

Hold the Volume through the End of a Sentence

WATCH VIDEO ON VOLUME AT END

WWW.EXECUTIVESPEAKINGINAWEEKEND.COM/VOLUMEATEND

Notice if your voice drops in volume while delivering the last words in sentences, especially in the Close. Instead, keep your volume strong so listeners do not miss any of your talk.

> **TIP**
>
> Ask a colleague to signal to you in a meeting when your volume drops. Soon, you will notice it yourself and adjust.

Too Loud

When you speak too loudly, listeners may think you are yelling at them. Speaking too loud is socially inappropriate and can cost you assignments or promotions.

Causes: if you were raised among people who are loud, that volume may seem normal. Or, you may have a mild hearing loss or partially blocked ear canals.

It can be awkward for people to bring up this subject. If you think you may be speaking too loudly, ask a trusted colleague to indicate during a meeting or conversation when you should lower your volume. Although it may seem too quiet, use this new volume consistently.

"I Speak too Fast."

WATCH VIDEO ON SLOWLY ENOUGH

WWW.EXECUTIVESPEAKINGINAWEEKEND.COM/SLOWLYENOUGH

"Whenyoupeakquickly,itsoundsthiswaytolisteners."
("When you speak quickly, it sounds this way to listeners.")

Why do you speak fast?

- You have always spoken fast and feel comfortable with it.
- You may be concerned that others will stop listening so you speak fast while you have their attention.
- You may speed up just to end the speaking agony sooner.
- Note: All people *think four times faster* than the speed at which others like to listen. Your speaking may be keeping pace with your thinking.

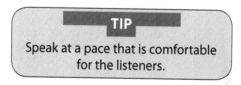

TIP

Speak at a pace that is comfortable for the listeners.

- The cost of speaking too quickly? Speaking too fast decreases listener's comprehension of your material, so you may have to repeat or explain misunderstandings. Therefore, during meetings and telephone calls, ask a friend to remind you to speak slowly.
- When fast speakers slow their pace of speaking, they usually still speak too quickly! Therefore, speak.... in..... a.... way... that.... seems... too....slow. That will probably be correct pacing for you.
- Do not write so much material that your self-talk says, "I have so much to say, I need to hurry up!" It is

actually best to prepare 10% less material than the time allotted so you don't feel rushed.

- Speaking slower actually lowers *your own* speaking stress.

Appear Smarter, more Competent and of Higher Status

Pronounce each sound in each word completely. Say, "working" not "workin'." Don't delete a final S or Z sound. Don't mumble (not clearly distinguishing sounds).

This very small adjustment will immediately have people perceive you as more educated and more accomplished.

Use Belly Breathing (Diaphragmatic Breathing)

- Do you run out of air before completing a sentence?
- Do your neck, throat and shoulders hurt at the end of the day just from speaking?
- Do you breathe shallowly or gasp for air when you are anxious?

Most people breathe using one third of the available space in their lungs. With limited air intake you may run out of air before completing a thought. You may be employing your neck, throat and shoulders to push out that little bit of air.

Belly breathing is the antidote. It is lowering the body's diaphragm to fill lungs more fully with air.

How to Belly Breathe

- Notice a baby's belly as it sleeps. It goes up and down as the lungs fill completely with air. This is how you breathe as you sleep.
- To learn belly breathing: when you awaken, observe that your belly rises and falls, just like a baby's. Analyze which muscles you use so you can call on them to belly breathe whenever you want.
- When belly breathing, the only movements are your stomach muscles pulling in and your vocal chords vibrating. Relax your neck and shoulders.
- During a presentation, take a belly breath after you reveal a new screen or after you ask people to look at a page in the handout. Since they are reading, you have a moment to take this breath as you look at your notes.

Behaviors to Avoid

Avoid Sarcasm

Sarcasm is hostile behavior. As fun as it is to be sarcastic, people respond with anger because you have been aggressive with them. They stop listening to you.

Sarcasm comes from the tone and the loudness you use with certain words. The sentence, "I am sure you got it right." will sound sarcastic when said, "I am **sure you** got it *right.*"

People trust you less when you use sarcasm. They are wary you will use it to embarrass them in front of colleagues.

WATCH VIDEO ON *NO SARCASM*

WWW.EXECUTIVESPEAKINGINAWEEKEND.COM/NOSARCASM

The Alternative

When something bothers you, tell the person quickly and to resolve the issue resolved without resorting to sarcasm. Do this privately or during a meeting. Rehearse so that you use neutral words and voice.

Avoid Upspeak

Definition of Upspeak: A statement that sounds like a question.

As in other languages, American English has a predictable musical sound:

- In American English, sentences begin on a high tone of the musical scale and end on a low tone scale and end low.
- Questions end on a higher tone on the scale than the rest of the sentence.
- "Upspeak" makes sentences sound like questions.
- *Upspeak weakens the validity and strength of your message*

WATCH VIDEO ON AVOID UPSPEAK

WWW.EXECUTIVESPEAKINGINAWEEKEND.COM/AVOIDUPSPEAK

The Antidote

Identify a friend or colleague who loves music - that person has the auditory skills to recognize upspeak. Have that person instruct you in this two-step process:

1. First, have them train your ear to hear Upspeak. Ask your friend to say statements, sometimes with the final tone ending low and sometimes ending up like a question. You identify which sentence is said properly and which is said with upspeak.
2. Next, you say statements and have your friend/colleague catch and correct upspeak.

Avoid Repeating Sound Patterns

When first speaking or when reciting a list, some people use a sound pattern repeatedly. Listeners either pay attention to the musical tones and not the content, or they stop listening completely.

Using a repetitious sound pattern at the start of a talk is interpreted by the listeners as nervousness. The antidote is to deliver the first five minutes of any talk with an animated voice, Voice Variety, that matches the meaning of the words.

WATCH VIDEO ON *AVOID SOUND PATTERNS*

WWW.EXECUTIVESPEAKINGINAWEEKEND.COM/AVOIDSOUNDPATTERNS

Control "Um, Uh, Er, You know, Like, Actually, Literally, Basically" and other Filler Words

Get comfortable with *silence* instead of using a filler word

- Pause for a second between sentences.
- Use silence when you look away to remember or develop an idea.
- Use silence as you check your notes.

> **TIP**
>
> Occasionally when you strategically use silence, someone interrupts and starts talking! Stop using pauses when speaking with them.

Voice Variety

Vary your loudness, tone and pace to highlight important ideas.

When you speak in a monotone (you sound the same no matter what you say), *you leave it to the listeners to decide which parts of your talk are most important.*

Instead, *identify highlights for them* by modifying your voice as you deliver significant ideas.

WATCH VIDEO ON VOICE VARIETY

WWW.EXECUTIVESPEAKINGINAWEEKEND.COM/VOICEVARIETY

You probably already emphasize certain numbers, dates and phrases by saying them LOUDER than the rest of the material. Although the listeners are not be aware of it, your voice has emphasized key ideas.

> **TIP**
> Since listeners do not listen to everything you say, use Voice Variety to alert them to noteworthy points.

Voice Variety Techniques

- Each Voice Variety technique below needs to be exaggerated to be noticed. Speak normally, though, in other parts of the sentence.

- You may be concerned that using your voice in these extreme ways will seem fake and contrived or that people will notice and think it odd. If you use an *assortment* of Voice Variety techniques, they will not notice. What you will notice, however, is that they take home more of your information.

Apply Voice Variety

For example, you may want the listeners hear that the **32% increase** was a significant improvement in the first quarter of the year. The full sentence might be, "We are happy to report that there was a 32% increase in the first quarter."

However, the notes to remind you what to say will have only the cue and significant words on them. Do not write full sentences!

Notes should look like this:

- ↑32%   1st Q

But these notes do not emphasize 32%

To emphasize 32%, you have choices:

Louder

If you choose to say 32% LOUDER, use a large bold font on your notes to remind yourself to increase your volume:

- ↑**32%**   1st Q

More Quietly

If you choose to say 32% quietly, use a small font on your notes:

- ↑32%   1ˢᵗ Q

> **TIP**
>
> **Notes remind you *what* to say and, with Voice variety, *how* to say it.**

Other Voice Variety Techniques

It is a mistake to use only one or two Voice Variety techniques. There are many more.

What has the same impact as LOUD and QUIET?

Pause After an important idea to allow time for the idea to be "downloaded."

Use a large double slash, in a different color than your notes, to indicate a pause:

- ↑32%**//**   1ˢᵗ Q

Pause Before an important idea to bring attention to that point.

When you pause *before* something significant, people really listen to what said next. Create a visual cue on your notes:

- ↑ **//** 32%   1ˢᵗ Q

Make your *voice Go Up or Down in Pitch* while saying a key idea; the unusual musical sound makes it stand out.

For example: If you played the notes on a piano which match the musical pitches you use in normal conversation, you probably would play five to seven notes in the center of the keyboard.

By speaking on a note that is much higher up or much lower down on the keyboard on a significant point, that idea will stand out from the rest of the material.

Design reminder to use a Higher Tone:

To remember to use a higher tone:

- ↑32%   1ˢᵗ Q

Or a Lower Tone:

- ↑32%   1ˢᵗ Q

Say it Very Slowly or Repeat It

These two techniques make the most impact but are also the most annoying when overused.

Therefore, use these *infrequently* and only for major points.

Your notes indicate the voice change:

Say the 32% Slowly:

- ↑ 3 2 % 1st Q

Or Repeat 32%:

- ↑32%...32% 1st Q

Combine Techniques

Combine two Voice Variety techniques. The more variations you use, the less identifiable they will be to your listeners.

Use LOUD + Pause After

- ↑**32%//** 1st Q

Use Pause Before and Quiet

- ↑**//** 32% 1st Q

Which Voice Variety to use?

In rehearsal, try out *all* of the Voice Variety techniques and combinations. Use what best matches each idea.

Mistakes made with Voice Variety

- Do not use one or two of the techniques exclusively. Listeners will notice and pay attention to them rather than to your material.
- Be careful not to pause too frequently.
- Some people do not deliver Voice Variety noticeably enough. For example: be sure to say the LOUD very loud and make pauses last for the count of three.
- It is not a good idea to emphasize everything in a sentence - nothing will stand out if everything is said dramatically. Speak in a normal conversational way except for the Voice Variety choices.

On the Telephone, Teleconferences and Webinars

- Your voice is your main tool used during teleconferences and webinars.
- Have you noticed how a speaker with a monotone delivery loses listeners' interest? Your use of Voice Variety will keep participants engaged.
- During the meeting surround yourself with notes that include obvious Voice Variety notations.
- For important meetings or projects, rehearse aloud the sentences containing Voice Variety as well as the Opener and Close.

How to improve Visuals and Voice:

1. Choose one body language and a voice behavior to incorporate it into your regular speaking style for a week.
2. The next week, choose to use another body language and voice skill. Continue this pattern.
3. Your new behaviors will soon become habits

CHAPTER 5

No-Stress Speaking

"You seem a little concerned about your talk."

Fear of speaking is normal. Anxiety is not.

It is our thoughts that escalate normal speaking fear into anxiety. Anxiety comes from what we tell ourselves about what happened in the past or what is going to happen.

Lower Speaking Anxiety

It is good to silently repeat any of these statements that are true for you:

- Fear is normal. It usually subsides after five minutes. I've practiced the first five minutes so I appear confident.
- I am only here to help them.
- I can do this.
- If someone else gave them this information, they would be just as satisfied. It is not about me.
- If I leave something out, they won't know because *they don't have my notes.* I can either leave it out or add it without apology.
- I will do the best I can.
- I have valuable information.
- I have good ideas.
- I don't have to rush through. I have prepared 10 minutes less material than the time given.
- I can ask for time to research a question that I can't answer.
- I can handle anything that comes up.
- This is not an exact science.
- I know what I'm talking about. (If you must deliver another person's material, prepare by asking what questions you may get and how to respond).
- It is not the electric chair.
- I probably won't be fired.
- I deserve to be here.
- I focus on my goal of transferring ideas and information, not my stress.

"But I still have anxious thoughts!"

When you notice your self-talk "Inner Critic's" thoughts, challenge and check them for accuracy. Re-write them with the truth. For example:

- ### *"I forget words/my mind goes blank."*
  Change this to, "On my notes I have written the words that were difficult for me during rehearsal." And "If I lose my place, I can review the last information given."

"I kept saying I'd die if I made a mistake during my talk."

- ### *"I will be humiliated if I make a mistake."*
  Adjust your thinking to, "I will make mistakes and fix them. I may feel bad."

- *"My whole career depends on this one talk."*

  Dispute this idea with, "I am prepared. I will do my best. They know my work; one talk won't change their opinion of me if I have a bad day. This is only one part of my job."

  "I have rehearsed and I have notes. Others have listened to portions of my talk and have given me constructive feedback."

> **TIP**
>
> Notice your Inner Critic's undermining thoughts because if you do not, you may be vulnerable to its subtle harassment.

I am not a fan of generic affirmations such as, "~~I will do great~~." The Inner Critic will usually not stop tormenting you as a result of a general thought like that. It is better to notice and debate your own personal thoughts.

More Ideas to Lower Stress

- Have a picture of your children or your pet on your notes to remind yourself there is more to your life than this one talk.
- Remember compliments you have received. Keep in mind good speaking experiences.
- Re-write bad speaking memories: see yourself as how you *wish* you had done it. This will help you behave in

your preferred way the next time a similar situation occurs.

- Imagine the group appreciating you because they sense you want to help them.
- Because speaking is a physical workout, warm up by taking a walk before your talk.
- Use music to relax or energize you. Listen to favorite music before speaking.
- Stretch your body; do mouth exercises (open your mouth, scrunch up your face, stick out your tongue) and move your neck and arms. Take an exercise or yoga class to learn how to tighten and relax muscles just before it is your turn to speak.
- Clear your mind. Count to four while breathing in, hold your breath for four counts and breathe out to the count of four. Repeat. You can do this before you speak - without anyone realizing it.
- Since most of the time your performance has been up to standards, odds are in your favor you will do well again.
- Many people feel they are impostors – "I know I do my work every day but if people realized how I only just pull it together, they would know I am a fraud." Everyone feels that way at some time. If you get the job done then you are the capable, skilled person you appear to be. You probably have evidence that you are a competent person who should be speaking to these people. Remind yourself of reality!

What *Not to do* to Lower Speaking Stress

Have you ever suddenly, midweek, had the urge to drink, use drugs, eat, sleep, gamble, watch lots of TV, play hours of video games, stay on the computer, or shop?

These are ways to cope with stress, but not good ways. These start as bad habits that help us feel better. However, these are in a different category than bad habits; these are addictions because they turn against us and we can't stop the obsessive / compulsive thoughts and behaviors. They can ruin professional and personal lives.

Obsessive thoughts about any of these desires last between eight and 15 minutes. If you can distract yourself, the cravings will pass. Stop and ask yourself, "Why do I want to self-medicate? Why do I want to go unconscious?" "I have that talk coming up! Preparation will make me feel better."

A Better Choice

The only person who can help an addict is another addict who is "recovereing" from the dependency of needing to do that behavior when stressed.

If you know someone who has gotten hooked by an addiction, let them know that they can attend the free meetings of AA (Alcoholics Anonymous), NA (Narcotics Anonymous), DA (Debtors Anonymous), OA (Overeaters Anonymous), etc. There will be a listing of telephone, online and in-person meetings on each site. There is a self-test on www.aa.org. Take it (substitute your potential addiction for the word alcohol) to see if you or a friend might be a candidate for getting help.

> **TIP**
> Aim for progress and small improvements
> each time you speak, not perfection.

Medicine for Speaking Stress

Although there is medicine for lowering stress, you won't be able to use it when someone spontaneously turns to you and says, "Why don't you give us an update."

It is better to learn to control your own stress using the suggested techniques.

© Randy Glasbergen
glasbergen.com

"I think my spell-checker is broken. It keeps
changing l-u-c-k to p-r-e-p-a-r-a-t-i-o-n."

Lower Stress with Preparation

Research the Listeners' Preferences

By calling ahead with Audience Analysis (covered in another chapter), you will discover what information they want and if they want an overview or details.

Ask Trusted Friends to Watch a Rehearsal

Explain the purpose and goals of the talk. Ask friends to interrupt your rehearsal with constructive feedback on content and delivery.

Expect to be Challenged

- What are the questions you don't want to hear? Who are the difficult people you may see? Ask colleagues for suggestions on how to respond and behave.
- Write every concern you have about equipment, software and all else that could go wrong. Next to each one, write what you will do if that happens.

> **TIP**
>
> People who are habitually stressed when speaking often say they don't take time to prepare. However, *that is why they are stressed.*

Lower Stress *Before* the Presentation

Go to the meeting room (or a similar room) beforehand, even the day before. Give your talk aloud using the same voice and body language you will use in the real talk.

- Even when you have little preparation time, it is important to know what your first and last sentences will be. Say these aloud. *Just thinking about them is not rehearsing.*

- Belly breathe to inhale enough air to complete your thoughts.

Imagine it Going Well

Imagine yourself doing well. Pretend you are in a play with you acting the part of a confident speaker.

Allow No Distractions before your talk

- Arrive earlier than you think you should.
- Do not answer your phone or look at texts or email.
- Check that all audios and visuals are cued up and ready. Ask an audio/visual savvy friend to be ready to help if things go wrong.
- Greet people as they arrive to have familiar faces to connect with as you speak.
- Have notes as insurance. Although you may not use them, it lowers anxiety to know they are there.
- Set up a table for your laptop or notes. Stand near so you can easily read.

Lower Stress *During* the Presentation

When you Mouth Feels Dry

- You have time to sip water after you show a new visual or ask them to turn to another page.
- Visualize eating a lemon to make your mouth water.

When you make Mistakes

Do not bring attention to your mistake by saying, "Excuse me" or "Sorry." Give the correct information and continue speaking. Maintain your self-assured appearance.

When you Sense you are Losing their Attention

Stop and get feedback from them about what they want. Either give that information or explain why you should continue with your material.

Ask a question to know how to adjust. These special questions are called *tie downs*.

- What parts would you like me to clarify/explain further?
- See how this aligns with your/our plan?
- How would you apply this information?
- What parts would work and would not work for you?
- This makes sense, doesn't it?
- How would you adjust this?

After you Speak

- Evaluate what was effective. It is tempting to only notice what we did not like.

- "What did I learn to do/not do again?" Target those improvements in your daily speaking.

Speak When you are Afraid to Participate

Do you hesitate to participate during regular business meetings?

Have you declined important speaking invitations?

Most coworkers do not appreciate a non-participant. They want to know your preferences and, if they are fair, want to give you your way some of the time.

Not speaking up also suggests you consent to the ideas. "No Action = Acceptance"

When you decline larger speaking opportunities, either with you as the key speaker or as a participant with significant people in the organization, you limit your visibility and career growth possibilities.

"What if I say something stupid?"

- Of the last 100 times you have spoken, what percentage did you say something stupid? 50%? 20%? 5%? In reality, most of the time you do not say stupid things. Use this new self-talk, "I mostly have valuable ideas. The odds are in my favor that this idea will be respected, also."
- Watch the people who are unafraid to speak up. When they say something that is not accepted, they shrug

their shoulders and say, "Okay" or "Here is another idea." Imitate the people whose performance you admire.

"I do not want to be aggressive."

- Have you seen truly aggressive people? Are you truly aggressive? If you do not match that anti-social behavior, then over-ride your fear and show that you have good ideas, too.
- Assert yourself to feel proud of yourself.
- If you rarely speak, just talking with normal assertiveness may make you feel as if you are being aggressive. Check with a colleague to see if you are acting inappropriately.

"They are so much more important than I am."

- You were invited by upper management or colleagues because you belong in the discussion.
- They may have fancier titles or make more money than you do, but they value your adding your opinion and ideas.

"Others argue. I don't like to argue."

- Defending your position is not arguing. Walk into the meeting prepared with all of the reasons why your idea has value. Anticipate their objections and how you will answer.
- Often, people argue, speak loud and interrupt as a means of getting their own way.
- Serve the organization by speaking when you know your ideas have merit.

"Others don't like it when I disagree."

Having a difference of opinion does not cause people to lose respect for you. Drop the "disease to please." You risk becoming easy to manipulate if you try too hard to gain everyone's approval.

"I'm shy." "I wasn't raised to speak up; it is unfamiliar."

- It is fine to be shy... *at home.*
- At *work*, you must speak up. Ask the communicators you admire to mentor you in participating.
- You see yourself as shy. However, your colleagues may see you as not wanting to share your value with the group or as selfishly or inappropriately holding back. Knowing how they view your behavior, isn't it better to go past your fear and participate?

Eliminate Apologetic Statements

- "I just..."
- "...you know?"
- "I only..."
- "May I ask..."
- "This may be dumb, but..."
- "..., okay?"
- "..., right?"
- "Does that make sense?" (repeatedly)
- "I'm sorry." (overused; truly apologize if you need to)
- "I kind of..."
- Or giggling

CHAPTER 6

Write to Match Each Group

"I wrote a great talk but they still looked bored."

"How do I adjust the material when I deliver the same ideas to various groups such as bosses, new hires or customers?"

"I know I give too much detail, but I want them to understand it all."

Connect with Various Groups

Use this chapter to prepare for any talk in which you want to influence, persuade, inspire or motivate.

Step by Step: Research the Audience, Construct and Edit your Talk, Be Interesting, Format, Write an Opener and a Close, Deal with Special Challenges and Add Transitions

Research the Audience Before you Write your Talk

It is beneficial to call the person who invited you to ask questions about what the group wants to receive from you.

You may ask: *"What could possibly motivate me to use my valuable time to make a research call that I don't want to make?"*

Answer: *Because their answers will write your talk for you!*

Make a Telephone Appointment to Interview the Contact Person

Who invited you to speak? An important member of the group, or someone from the support staff? Your boss? A colleague asking you to be the resource person?

If your Contact Person is an Important Member of the Group

As soon as you have identified this key person, call to make a telephone appointment. Have your questions already printed just in case this person is willing to be interviewed on this initial call. Ask the Audience Analysis Questions that appear later in this chapter.

The Script

- Establish your credibility: say your name and your company name v e r y   s l o w l y. Identify yourself as the "speaker for next Wednesday's meeting."

- Say who told you to call.
- Your professionalism with these first few sentences will indicate that their speaking with you will not be a waste of their time.

"I would like to speak with you for a few minutes to make sure my talk on Wednesday will be valuable for your people."

"May we set up a telephone appointment?" Is there a good time this week or next?"

If the Contact Person is part of the Support Staff

Begin with the same introduction. Explain that you "want to be prepared to give people the information that would be most useful" and ask that he/she set up a telephone appointment for you with a member of the group.

Be sincerely appreciative. Although he/she may not mention to anyone that you were polite, rudeness and impatience will be reported.

The Boss or a Colleague

Ask relevant Audience Analysis questions from the following:

You now have a Co-writer

Once you have a key person's attention, ask **Audience Analysis** questions. With each answer, note what to include in the talk.

Ask each question casually and encourage their thinking. Make it a positive experience for them.

- Be careful here not to supply answers; let your contact person talk.
- You can paraphrase (rephrase) what was said to make sure you understand.
- It is fine to ask more questions and politely push back when something seems vague.

Audience Analysis Questions

Prior to the call, create a document with questions that will help you personalize each talk. You will improvise some questions during the call, of course, but please respect their time and yours by preparing research questions.

- What would you like people to walk away with when I am finished speaking on Wednesday?
- Who is going to be there? Technical people? A mixed group of different technical people? Technical and non-technical? (Example: I.T. and marketing together, lucky you!)
- Are people familiar with our product or service? Unfamiliar?
- Experienced with our product or service? Not experienced?
- Do they like our product or service?
- What don't they like about our product or service? Specifically, what is it that they do not like? (Find out now and not be surprised when you get there.)
- What are they most interested in hearing about?

- How do you think I could be most valuable to the group?
- *Is there something you would like me to tell your group?*
- How many people will be there?
- How large is the room?
- If it is a large room, what is the layout of the tables/chairs? (You may be asked for your preference.)
- Will they provide a small table for a laptop?
- Will I be speaking at a conference table?
- Will I be sitting at the head of the table or on the side?
- Do they expect PowerPoint or handouts?
- What time am I scheduled to speak?
- Are there speakers before me? How many? What are their topics?
- Who will be providing audio/visual (A/V) assistance?
- How I get into the building? Will they leave my name at security? Who should I call if I have difficulty getting in?
- How early may I get into the room?

"You want me to say THAT in my talk?!"

More Analysis

At the end of your call, ask for the names of two more key people or participants.

Script: "You mentioned that there will be technical and non-technical people there (or experienced and non-experienced, or whatever the group mix). Would you give me the names of someone from each of those groups? I would like to ask them these questions to make sure I really give people what they're looking for on Wednesday."

You will easily get other participant's names and telephone numbers from your first contact person who will be impressed with your commitment to preparation.

> **TIP**
>
> Participants appreciate that you customized your program for them.

Get the Most Accurate Information

- Don't use e-mail for research - people either don't respond or they will send an inadequate answer.
- On the phone: when you ask, "Are people satisfied with what we're doing?" and you hear a singsong, "Well...uh, yes" you know that they are *not happy* with what we're doing! Push back and ask more questions. You would not get those subtle cues from an e-mail response.
- Call early, late or at lunchtime to reach the people.
- After you have spoken to the other two people, you will see a pattern of what the group really wants and

needs to hear. Do not depend on one person's point of view.

Construct and Edit Your Talk

Write your Talk from Research Results

Three Main Points

From the Audience Analysis, you may often find that their desired information falls in three main categories.

Are there always three? No. Sometimes there are two main points; sometimes there are 18.

Speakers frequently use three because human beings remember sets of three easily. Work with this natural inclination.

When you teach all day, have three take-away ideas for each section.

> **TIP**
>
> Be sure that your talk includes what *the listeners* care about (their "Hot Buttons" from Audience Analysis), not all that *you* care about.

Begin in the Middle (the Body) of the Talk

Create your talk by writing the names of the three main points/topics as bullets on paper or a screen. Put some space between each. Use this outline format to collect your ideas.

- Main Point 1

- Main Point 2

- Main Point 3

Brainstorm

Under each of these topics, list sub-bullets with as many ways that you can think of to explain those main points. Allow yourself to jump from one point to another as you think of ideas.

Write each idea without allowing any positive or negative judgment to stop you (Example: "This is the best idea I've ever had" or "This won't work"). Even if an idea seems mediocre, add it anyway. The next day when you open this document, that mediocre idea many spark a brilliant one.

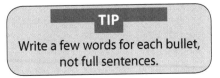

TIP
Write a few words for each bullet,
not full sentences.

Do not edit your thinking yet. That comes later. Editing too early will limit your creativity.

The goal here is to capture everything you can think of. Ask colleagues for input. The goal is to *write too many ideas*.

Help Yourself

Begin this process as soon as you know you will be speaking. Why? You will notice how others explain these concepts. You will notice examples, stories and analogies that might work well for you.

EDIT your Material

After achieving your goal of brainstorming (having too many ideas), edit your information. Saying every idea listed in your brainstorming would waste listeners' time.

Label each sub-bullet:

- **"N"**

  Identify the few things that listeners need to know when they walk out after the talk. Place an "N" for "Need to Know" by those items.

- **"SH"**

  "I should also tell them." These are the items that are not as important as the "Needs to know" but you feel you should mention them.

- **"I"**

  For all that remain, put "I" for "I would like them to know." For example, "I would like you to know that I worked three weeks on this for you" (No, just kidding.)

Now, every item on your brainstorming list is labeled "N" "SH" or "I."

The Final Editing Step

- *Select only the "Need to Know" items and copy them to a new document. These, and only these, will be your talk.*
- You may want to take the "Should tell them" and "I would like them to know" information in a handout or place them on a hidden page in PowerPoint in case someone is interested. You can cover that information with the person after your meeting.

TIP

Your listeners are experts in their own fields.
They do not want to be experts in your field.
Give them the answers they want.

Be Interesting

Interact with listeners: Use "Supports" with Facts

For example: Ron, the Quality Control VP for an international pharmaceutical company, takes a sample from every batch of drugs produced at his manufacturing plant and puts these into containers in large refrigerated units. During a storm, the electricity to the refrigerated units was off for six hours. The back-up generators had not worked.

Luckily, there was no significant change in the temperature of the samples. No damage was done.

Three days after the power failure, a U.S. Food and Drug Administration representative arrived to inspect the plant. The news about the power outage shocked him. He hinted that the drugs involved would have to be recalled from around the world, causing a multi-million-dollar loss.

The scientists and researchers stated facts, facts and more facts - verifying no significant change in temperature and that this was a non-issue. None of these facts affected the FDA representative.

Ron spoke. "I live nearby. The electricity in our home went off for six hours also. I had beer in a cooler in the refrigerator and even though the refrigeration was off, there was no significant change in the temperature in the beer."

The FDA representative first looked disgusted, then softened his face and said, "OK" and moved on to the next topic.

He finally understood because of an *analogy*, not facts.

Please notice two things:

1. An analogy influenced him to consider the idea.
2. Did you, like him, imagine the beer in the refrigerator, and see the man's face change?

The pictures probably appeared on the movie screen inside of your brain. *That is the power and the reason to use analogies and other "Supports" with your material.*

Have Your Ideas Seen inside of Their Brains

- Facts fly past people's ears - your listeners may or may not invite them into their brains.
- But *you* can make your ideas appear as pictures to them by using Supports to reinforce your material.
- Supports are the added examples, questions, quotations, etc. that make your material attention-getting and memorable.
- Supports make you a charismatic speaker.

How do Supports Capture their Attention?

If you only use facts, your listeners may get bored. The brain is has different areas processing stories, numbers, analogies, etc. For example, when you tell a story, the most primitive part of the brain is activated.

When you use different Supports, people spontaneously leave their own thoughts to pay attention to you.

List of Supports

- **Benefits to them** - State how your idea, product or service will make their lives better, make/save money, give them visibility, etc.
- **"Imagine"** – Describe what it will be like when they do what you suggest, or what it will be like if they don't.

- **Analogies, Metaphors, Similes** - Start with something known to them and link/bridge it to your new idea.
- **Stories** - From business or personal life
- **Examples** - Business or personal
- **Quotations** - Do an Internet search on "Business Quotations." Save any quotations that you may use in upcoming talks. (Quotations are the only thing written out fully in your notes, with dynamic Voice Variety.)
  - When you quote people who are well known in your field or respected in the world, you effortlessly borrow some of their power.
  - You can quote people from your personal life, too.
- **A folk tale from your childhood** - People usually like to know more about your history, especially if you were raised in another country.
- **Rhetorical Questions** - Ask a question and answer it.
- **Survey Questions** - Ask if people are familiar with, use, like, don't like something, etc. (Do not insult people by using obvious and patronizing questions like, "Who would like to make more money?")
  - Hold your hand high up to model how they should vote.
  - People want to know the outcome of your survey. Calculate and then report: "It looks like one-third of the group," or "Almost everyone," or "Only a few."
- **An Unusual Statement or Statistic** - Be sure to use Voice Variety to make it more noticeable than the rest of the sentence.
- **Acronym** - Use a company word or any word that is easy to remember. For example, a SMART goal stands

for Specific, Measurable, Achievable, Relevant/Realistic and on a Timetable.

- **A current event** – Some speakers hold the morning paper and refer to an article with, "Let's make sure this doesn't happen here." or, "We can do this, too."
  Put the paper down after referring to it so that you don't shake it as you continue speaking.

- **Tie downs** - Stop to assess their comprehension. "Does this make sense?" "Should I continue?" "Have I made this idea clear?"

- **Humor** - Do not feel you must use humor. If you do want to lighten things up, use a humorous quotation that perfectly makes your point. Humor is risky. Always try humor on colleagues to get approval before using it.

You probably Use Supports Already

- You most likely use Supports, *randomly*.
  - When you go to parties, you may explain what you do for work by using analogies.
  - Think of how you already use examples and stories to persuade people.

- Using Supports randomly makes you a good speaker. But to be a great speaker, purposely *pre-choose* to add Supports to your material. Rehearse them aloud, make them succinct, and add Voice Variety.

- Do not become known as "the story guy" or "the quotation lady" because you are only comfortable with a couple of Support categories. Have others help you get skilled at using each type of Support list for maximum effect.

Where can you find Supports?

Your co-workers already use stories, examples, quotations, questions and analogies to explain your work issues. People from related departments explain what you and your department do by using Supports. Often it is the person completely unrelated to your work who suggests the freshest ideas.

Ask others to help you add Supports to your talk

1. Tell each person:
    - Who you will be speaking to
    - The topic
    - The action you want the group to take when you are finished
    - Your three main points
2. Show them the list of Supports. They will suggest examples, analogies or quotations, etc. for each of your main points.

Your Daily Experiences can become Supports

For example: I told the roofer who completed the job on my house that he did a great job.

He said, *"Everyone has time to do a job over. But no one has time to do it right the first time."*

I use that quotation to great effect when colleagues are tempted to jump into something without adequate preparation or research.

Customize Supports to the Listeners

For example:

Ben represents the National Institute of Health when he speaks to U.S. Congressional committees to ask for funding.

He tells them stories. They give him the money. *Every time.*

When asked, he stated, "That's what I do. I tell them stories and they give me the money."

Why does that work?

When he addresses them, he doesn't use physician's language because they are not doctors. He does not talk science because they are not scientists. He speaks about health issues that they can understand and relate to and says, "And this is what we will be working on." or, "This is the issue that deserves investigating."

Decide to Use or Not Use a Support

Ask trusted colleagues if your Supports are perfectly congruent with the points you are making. Ask them to coach you to deliver ideas concisely.

"My material is too complicated, dull or boring to add Supports."

No it isn't.

For example: Before I started their seminar, a company president told me what their company produced. This was the interaction:

"Have you ever made a cake?"

"Yes," I said.

"You know when you make a cake you have a layer of cake, icing on it and have another layer of cake and put a jelly layer on it and have another layer of cake and put icing on the top?"

"Yes."

"That is how we make computer chips. Then we carve down to whichever layers we need."

You may think your product or service is too complicated to explain to inexperienced people. But this president explained how to make computer chips using *cake*.

"Should I use Supports each and every time I speak?"

No. At the weekly update meeting, usually just report highlights of the data using Voice Variety. But when you want to convince, persuade and motivate, add Supports.

Techniques for Using Supports

You may be thinking, "I work with people who will laugh me out of the room if I start telling a story or quotation."

They *will* appreciate Supports if you use the proper techniques:

- Do not announce, "I want to tell you a story." or "There is a quotation that really fits what I am trying to say." Just begin saying the story or quotation - and notice how they become engaged.

- Especially don't say, "I want to tell you a funny story/ quotation." because no matter how funny it is, it is not as funny as they were expecting it to be.

Important: Bridge/Link the Support to your Material

Help the listener to see the connection.

For example, after saying a Support, say,

- "It is for this reason that we..."
- "I feel the same way about..."
- "That is what we intend to use this for."
- "Why is this important to us?"
- "How could this have happened?"
- "We don't want to do that again."
- "It seems to me that..."
- "We expect the same result this time, too."
- "We expect it will be different this time."
- "This is similar to..."
- "How is this similar to....?"
- "This is why we..."

Use Listener Participation

The trend in speaking is to invite listeners to discuss your ideas in pairs or small groups.

Why get listeners Actively Involved?

- To keep them interested

- To keep them awake in the afternoon or when you are the 4th or 5th speaker
- To find their objections and answer them before they become deal breakers
- To have your supporters positively influence those who object to your ideas

The Script

Pause in your lecture and ask for their participation:

"Please turn to the person next to you (or a few people near you) and...

- ...say how you can use this on your job."
- ...come up with what else needs to be done/discussed/developed."
- ...discuss how this will help our department/project."

Regaining Attention after the Group Discussion

If you have asked the group to discuss something and want their attention back on you, loudly say,

1. "30 second warning."
2. Wait another 30-45 seconds.
3. Say, "Please come back."
4. Do not speak until there is silence. If you begin while someone else is still speaking, you are indicating that it is fine with you that they talk while you are talking.

Format Your Talk

Organize from the Middle Outward

Imagine books on a bookshelf. The Need-to-know Main Points are the books. They are the Body of the talk.

It is optional to use bookends on each side of the books, similar to the optional Preview and Review summaries.

The important Opener and influential Close are like flowers on one side of the books and a plant on the other.

The outline of the Body of the talk looks like this:

* **Main Point 1**
    *
    *
    *
 * **Main Point 2**
    *
    *
 * **Main Point 3**
    *
    *

Alternatives for "Main Points 1, 2, and 3" are:

- Problem
- Solution

- Problem
- Solution

- Etc.

or

- Their question
- The answer

- Their question
- The answer

- Etc.

or

- Comparisons with Pro and Con columns

or

- Any configuration that helps the listeners to easily understand

Optional Preview/Review Summaries

Decide if your listeners would find it valuable to hear a Preview Summary (Agenda) prior to the Body of the talk, and/or a Review Summary after the Body.

The choice is always based on what would best aid comprehension. For example, newly hired employees would find both a Preview and Review valuable, while coworkers may not find either valuable.

Use one, both or neither.

The outline of the Body + Optional Preview and Review of the talk looks like this:

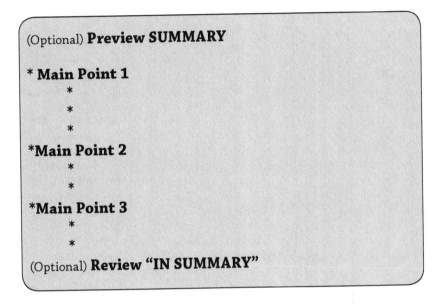

(Optional) **Preview SUMMARY**

* Main Point 1
   *
   *
   *

*Main Point 2
   *
   *

*Main Point 3
   *
   *

(Optional) **Review "IN SUMMARY"**

Write Attention-Getting Openers and Motivational Closes

WATCH VIDEO ON OPENER AND CLOSE

WWW.**E**XECUTIVE**S**PEAKING**I**N**A**W**EEKEND**.COM/**O**PENERAND**C**LOSE

- **The Opener** - This gathers listeners' attention. The Opener is consistent with the ideas in the Body of the talk.

- **The Close** - End by stating clearly what action you want the listeners to take. For example, ask them to sign something, or to just be familiar with what your organization can do for them, set an appointment, etc.

Why use an Opener?

- When you begin to speak to any group, people are thinking about many things... but not you! When you open in an interesting way, they will look up from email and phones to give their attention to you.
- You particularly need an Opener that commands attention when you speak in the afternoon or after several other speakers.

Openers should be simple. Make them more engaging when you:

- present an important project
- speak with key people
- speak on teleconferences, since you need to do everything you can to gain and maintain their attention

Customize Openers

Look at your audience's website to incorporate their specifics into your Opener.

Quote someone significant in the organization by saying, "I noticed in your annual report (or Mission Statement or in an article) that Joe Smith established the importance of X, Y and Z. I am going to address how we can be helpful to you in reaching those goals."

Why use a Close?

- People often end a talk with a Review Summary of the material. *This does not ask listeners to do what you want them to do.*
- A Close incorporates a 'call to action."
- *Always* announce the Close ("In closing..." or "The bottom line is...") to get them to hear what action you want them to take.

"Should I always use an Opener and Close?"

You do not need an Opener or Close when delivering your weekly numbers or updates.

The Opener and Close are SUPPORTS

When you open with something intriguing, you capture the listeners' attention more than opening with facts alone.

The Close, if it is interesting, holds their interest as you deliver the request or motivational thought.

Optional "Purpose Statement"

- **After the Opener**, you could add motivation to listen by saying, "The purpose of my talk is to ..." when you know you are meeting one or more of their needs.
- This is also the time to insert, "Thank you for inviting us," if you choose to say that.

- You might introduce yourself or announce who will be speaking on which topics. This is the place to tell them to ask questions as you present or to hold them until the end.

Write the Opener, Close (and optional Purpose)
Leave a space for taking questions

The outline of the talk looks like this:

OPENER - An easy to remember Support. Use 100% EYE CONTACT (Grab their attention!)

(Optional) **PURPOSE** Benefits to them
(Introduce yourself / Announcements / Ask questions or hold them until the end / Thank you / What they will learn from you and how you will help them)

(Optional) **Preview SUMMARY**
* Main Point 1
    *
    *
    *

*Main Point 2
    *
    *

*Main Point 3
    *
    *

(Optional) **Review "IN SUMMARY"**

Q & A

"IN CLOSING… - Use an easy to remember Support. 100% EYE CONTACT (This is where you ask them act on something.)

// (pause for 5 seconds)

WATCH VIDEO ON OPENER AND CLOSE WITH EYE CONTACT

WWW.EXECUTIVESPEAKINGINAWEEKEND.COM/OPENERANDCLOSEWEYECONTACT

The Logistics of Using an Opener

- Deliver the Opener with 100% eye contact. It indicates that you want to connect and help them. They make the decision to listen in those first few seconds. Therefore, write a brief Opener that is easy for you to remember.

- Rehearse it aloud so you will make a great first impression. Practice with the Voice Variety you will use.

- Follow the Opener with a transition to your material such as, *"This is just how we...."* or *"And that is why we..."* *"If we want this to happen/avoid this..." "Today I will address..."*

The Logistics of Using a Close

- ***Let people know the Close is coming*** when you anounce the Question and Answer period with a phrase such as, "Before I close, what questions do you have?" "If there are no more questions, let me end with this..." "In closing..." "I'd like to end with this..." "I will leave you with this..."
- Deliver the Close using eye contact and Voice Variety.
- Count to five silently to allow them to absorb the Close. Nod that you are finished. *Because this is the last thing they hear, they will walk out with your Close in their minds.*
- Do not end with, "Thank you" because we do not want them keeping "Thank you" in mind as they leave. If you want to thank them, say that in the Purpose Statement.

> **TIP**
>
> After the close, stop talking! Allow them to think about what you have asked them to do before nodding that you are finished.

Write Quickly and Easily

Use a Mind Map

Draw a circle in the center of a sheet of paper.

- Write in the circle the answers to these two questions:
    - ○ To whom are you speaking?
    - ○ What you want them to do when you finish speaking?
- Draw three circles to the side of the first one. In each of these circles, write the name of a Main Point that, if explained, would cause those people in the first circle to do what you want them to do.
- At the top of the page, open with a Support. For example, write about a time when something similar happened and say how your current talk is similar to this example. Or quote someone from the organization who addressed this topic.
- At the bottom of the page write, "In closing..." Write a Support to Close. For example, it could be a rhetorical question focusing on the benefits they will receive for doing what you suggest.
- Now, think of sub-points to add to each of the three Main Points. Each of these three circles will begin to look like a child's drawing of the sun - a circle with lines sticking out all from it. Your sub-points are written on these tangents.

This completes the Mind Map.

Although this is similar to as writing ideas in a list, i.e. main points with bullets below, sometimes this change in format stimulates thinking.

Mind Mapping software is available on the Internet. It takes time to input the information, but it looks terrific when printed out.

> **TIP**
>
> Some people like the Mind Map format so much that they use it as their notes for the actual talk.

Special Preparation Challenges

"How about Impromptu Speaking?"

You most frequently will be requested to speak on your areas of expertise. Use the template of Opener, bullets and Close. Open the talk. Surprisingly, your brain, thinking four times faster than you are speaking, will supply the first bullet, other bullets and the Close.

"I Suddenly have to Give a Talk to a Group."

Say the best Opener you can. Next, conduct an audience analysis by their show of hands to find what they need to know. Take questions as you go along or leave plenty of time for questions toward the end. Close.

"I must Deliver Another Person's Material."

If you frequently must fill in for others, ask those colleagues to keep you up to date on their projects. Even when the people must be away for an emergency, ask that they please answer your telephone calls.

1. Call the person to ask about the parts of their information that are not clear to you, especially charts and graphs.
2. Ask what questions you may be asked.
3. Ask for the answers to those questions.

Do not open your talk with, "I am not really the person who did this work or usually speaks about this, but I will do the best I can." That is announcing, "I intend to break Rule #1 and waste your time!"

Instead, begin with, "I am here to give you an overview/update you on _____. My colleague, Jessie, will be available later to go into detail for specific questions you have."

Do not be apologetic. When you do not know an answer, say, "I will ask Jessie about that and either she or I will get back to you."

"I'm not allowed to tell company secrets."

They know you know the information. To deny it will cost you credibility. Say,

> "I know that answer but I can't talk about it yet. As soon as I can, I will let you know."

Smooth Transitions between Points

Transitions are usually undervalued! They not only bridge one idea to the next, they also attract listeners' attention away from their own self-talk.

Use transitions to draw attention to what is important and help them see how each point contributes to the whole.

Choose the transition words you intend to use and *place them on your notes*. You will sound polished and articulate.

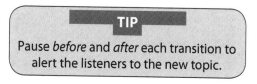

TIP

Pause *before* and *after* each transition to alert the listeners to the new topic.

Transition Words and Phrases

Next area and **In Addition** – With that in mind, Let's now look at, Next, Let's move on to, Now that we understand that the next issue is, Subsequently, Where do we go from here?, Simultaneously, We need to look at _____ as well, Also, Further, Furthermore, Still, Additionally, In addition, Besides, What's more, Moreover, Besides, Not only... but also

Time and **Numerical Order** - Until, At this time, Since, For the time being, Previously, At this point, At the same time, Later, Earlier, At an earlier time, In the past, formerly, In the future, Immediately, Meanwhile, In the meantime, Now, Currently, Temporarily, After a while, After that, Also, At last, Eventually, Finally, Last, Now, Afterward, First, Second, Third, At first, Originally, In the first place, Initially, To begin with, At the start, Eventually, Finally, Ultimately

Agenda and **Importance** – Here are three areas to consider, Our analysis results in these areas of concern, Let's look at the key areas today, Most importantly, Equally important, Exceeding, Beyond, Notice, Above all, Greater than, Moreover, Keep in mind, Over and above, Bear in mind, Similarly

Contrast/Compare and **Cause/Effect** – Including, Likewise, In the same way, Contrasting that, In contrast to, Excluding that, On the other hand, Like, Likewise, As well as, Both, Compared to, However, Conversely, By comparison, Instead, Nevertheless, Still, Apart from, Yet, If not, In opposition to, On the contrary, Otherwise, Not including, Neither... nor, As a result, Therefore, For this reason, For that reason, Consequently, Accordingly, Because of, Since, Due to, Given that, Seeing that, Then

Spatial Order - To the north, Alongside, Next to, To the left, Above, Moving eastward, In front of, Adjoining, Adjacent

Explanation - To illustrate, As an illustration, To clarify, To justify, Let's begin with, I'll start today with, I'll end today with, For example, As an example, For instance, Case in point, In other words, The reasoning behind, The thinking behind

Main Point – So what does all this mean? This leads us to one main idea, The best solution is, Here's the bottom line

Summary – To summarize, In summary, Now that you have all the information, Let's recap, What have we seen? Having considered all the data

Close: Ask for it – Finally, If you agree with this idea, Consequently, As a consequence, Last, Here's how we should move forward, The next step is, Therefore, Accordingly, What you need to do is, All in all, After all, Here's how we start, Allow me to suggest an action step, In closing, In conclusion, To conclude, I'll end today with..., The last thing I want to say is..., I will leave you with this...

CHAPTER 7

User-friendly Notes

User-Friendly Notes are the Scaffolding that Hold Up a Confident Speaker

Why use Notes?

- Notes are insurance against you losing your place, especially after an interruption.
- Notes eliminate thinking after a talk, "I left something out." or "I wish I had said the items in the order I had planned to use."
- Notes can stop you from rambling off the topic or giving too much detail.

The Format

- Use an outline or a Mind Map (described in the last chapter, *Write Quickly and Easily*).
- Write the fewest words possible that will remind you of what to say.
- Leave out any words or phrases your mind will automatically fill in:
  - There are many phrases, sentences, full paragraphs and even complete stories you frequently tell others. *Do not write them fully on your notes.* Make your notes cue/remind you of your ideas.
  - Delete all small words like: the, an, of, is, and, to, for, by, etc. because you will automatically say them.
- Color-highlight certain parts of your notes to help your eyes locate them.

> **TIP**
>
> Notes written in paragraph form guarantee that you will have difficulty finding your place.

Use Drawings and Symbols on Notes

The mind interprets drawings and symbols faster than words. Use them frequently on your notes.

- If you absolutely want to use a certain word, such as "increased," put that word on your notes. If you are equally happy to say, "went up," "improved," "moved in the direction we wanted," etc., it is efficient to use the symbol ↑ instead of writing out a word.

- When you want to say any of these words, "isn't, won't, can't, hasn't, never" or any word with a negation, use the symbol "X."
- You do not have to draw well. You only need to make sure *you* understand the cue.

Add Voice Variety indicators to your notes.

Your first set of notes will contain more words than your final version.

- As you rehearse aloud, try to delete unnecessary words from your notes.
- *Rehearse with your final set of notes to become familiar with where to look.*

"I have had notes but I've never used them!"

Your notes were probably not user-friendly and therefore not very helpful to you.

"I prefer to write out my entire talk."

If you resist the idea of using only an outline, it may be that you want to say each idea exactly as it is written, word for word. This results in your sounding as if you are reading or delivering a memorized talk - this does not engage listeners!

Deliver only the Opener and Close exactly as written. With rehearsal you will be able to explain each idea in the rest of your talk in a conversational way *because* of your abbreviated, user-friendly notes.

It is fine to use different wording each time you explain your ideas.

If you are a person who cannot think or create without writing your entire talk, here is the compromise:

Write your entire talk. When you have finished:

1. Say your talk aloud.
2. Take a yellow highlighter and highlight only the key ideas in each sentence.
3. Say your talk out loud again, but this time make your eyes go only from yellow highlight to yellow highlight as reminders of what to say.
4. Finally, copy only the yellow highlighted words as your next set of notes and give the talk again. The first time will be rough; the third and fourth times will be smoother. This is you final set of notes.

As long as you make your points and the listeners get the message, you have achieved your goal - transferring information.

"Even with minimal notes, I sound memorized, as if I am reading my talk."

Deliverthe Opener and Close with an animated voice that "acts out" their meaning.

To build confidence that you can deliver a line without memorization, rehearse the Body of the talk this way:

1. Glance at notes and deliver its message.
2. Say the same idea in another way.
3. Say the same idea in yet another way.

You will soon know you can rely on yourself to explain your ideas to others without memorization,

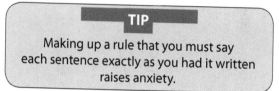

TIP
Making up a rule that you must say each sentence exactly as you had it written raises anxiety.

Where to put your notes

Try different forms and locations until you find the one most helpful to you.

Choices

- Print out the PowerPoint screens, three or six on a page. Next to each, remind yourself of what you would like to say.

  Either lay the printed notes on the table in front of you or hold them in one hand. Do not wave your papers as you speak.

- Use the *Notes* option of PowerPoint on the laptop screen. You will see what the audience sees plus your notes. The audience will not see your notes.

- Note cards - Number them, since they may fall out of your hands.
- When you speak to a webcam, put your notes on a flip chart pasted behind the camera. You will sound brilliant!

CHAPTER 8

Confidently Handle Questions and Answers

Handle yourself well in Q & A to strengthen your credibility

Anticipate Questions

At your next in-person or virtual meeting, what questions will you probably receive?

Most people can anticipate 75 - 80% of the questions they may encounter during a talk. Ask colleagues to add to this list.

- Have someone ask you each question. *Answer with a couple of sentences.* Have your friend coach you on responding succinctly.

- If you rehearse by yourself, still answer each question *aloud*.
  You will forget specific words or numbers that you want to include in a response - add those to your notes.
- Of course, you cannot anticipate every question. Your answer to an unanticipated question will not be as good as one that has been prepared, but you will probably sound knowledgeable since you speak about this information daily.
- Occasionally while practicing you will answer inappropriately! Be glad you rehearsed because you would have given that answer during your talk.
- Edit yourself as you practice if you usually give more detail than people want. Trust that if they want more information they will ask for it.
- If possible, rehearse answering questions in the real setting you will use or one that is similar. Speak using the same loudness, slow pacing and eye contact (to the empty chairs) that you will use in the real meeting.

Announce When you Prefer Taking Questions

You can choose to take questions throughout your talk or ask them to hold their questions until the end. Say your preference after the Opener.

Advantages and Disadvantages of Taking Questions during your Talk

Your goal is to keep listeners connected to you throughout your entire talk. Answering questions as they come up helps everyone to understand.

When you feel they are confused, stop and ask for questions.

The downsides are that the questions can use up your allotted time and that someone can attempt to dominate the discussion with too many questions.

Script for, "Please ask questions as I go along."

> "Please interrupt me to ask any questions. If I do not explain something clearly, please ask."

Raise your hand high as you say this to demonstrate what they should do. Otherwise they may raise hands to the level of their faces and you may not see them (and they get frustrated that you didn't call on them).

Answer briefly. They do not want you to give the talk again or give another talk. When you finish, ask if that answered the question.

Control the talk. When you get a question that will be handled in a few minutes say,

> "I will be covering that in a few minutes. If that does not answer your question, please ask again."

Obviously, *if the person who asks is the Boss*, you may answer it right away or say, "I will be getting to that point in a few minutes, but the short answer is..."

Advantages and Disadvantages of Holding Questions until the End

- You have better control of your timing.
- You can control the group dynamic - perhaps you have spoken to this group before and they asked so many questions you had to shorten your talk. Anticipate this as you prepare.
- The downside is some people may not understand an early point, causing them to not listen to the rest of your talk. This is addressed in the following script.

Script for, "Please hold questions until the end."

Even if you have chosen to have people wait until the end for questions, still include the opportunity to ask for clarification. After the Opener say,

> "Most of the questions I get on this material are included in my talk. Please hold your questions until the end. However, if I do not explain something clearly, of course ask for clarification."

WATCH VIDEO ON **Q & A**

WWW.EXECUTIVESPEAKINGINAWEEKEND.COM/QANDA

Template for Answering Questions

- As you reply, keep eye contact on the questioner for about five seconds. Look at other quadrants for five seconds to keep everyone's attention. End with your eyes back on the questioner. Ask,

  "Does that answer your question?" If the answer is, "Yes," allow the person another question. "Do you have another question?"

  After the second, "Does that answer your question?" look at a different part of the room and ask, "Who else has a question?"

Delete: "~~That's a good question.~~" "~~That's an interesting question.~~"

Do not begin your answer with a judgmental statement like this. It makes all the people who asked previous questions wonder, "Wasn't my question good? Wasn't my question interesting?"

Include All Participants

Take questions from each area in the room and from participants of all ranks and status.

"Should I end the talk with Q&A or the Close?"

- *End with the Close.* Why? One of the most important tools to take advantage of is that people remember the last thing they hear. Make your Close the last thing they hear.

- If you were to risk ending with their questions, the last question might be an unimportant, redundant or negative question. Then they would leave the room thinking of that interaction.
- Therefore, after the Body of the speech or after the Review Summary (if you use one) say,

  "Before I CLOSE, what questions do you have?" Say the word CLOSE very loud to make sure they know that something else is coming.

- Or, as you near the end of the Q & A time, say,

  "I will take two more questions and then I will CLOSE."

As soon as you have finished answering the last question,

- Do not pause!
- Do not say thank you!

After finishing the last question, immediately say, "IN CLOSING..., or "IN CONCUSION.... or "LET ME LEAVE YOU WITH THIS..." very loudly.

- Be silent as you look at your notes to remind yourself of the Close.
- Without looking at your notes again, deliver your Close with eye contact, a strong voice, Voice Variety and congruent facial movement.
- Stop talking, count to five silently (giving them time to comprehend your Close) and nod that you are finished.

Problems with Questions and Answers

"Our technical people miss the Close because they leave when I ask, 'What questions to you have?' They don't have questions and don't want to hear other's questions."

Write another Close to say after the last Main Point (or after the review summary). Say,

1. "IN CLOSING..." and deliver a Close.

2. Pause

3. Then say, "What questions do you have?"

    The technical people may get up and leave but you have Closed them; you have asked them to do what you want.

    The remaining people will hear the questions and answers. When you are finished with Q & A, alert them you are about to leave them with a final message.

    Say something like: "LET ME LEAVE YOU WITH THIS..." Deliver a new and different Close.

Do not say, "Again..." or "As I said before..." and repeat the same Close. This is because when people hear, "Again..." they stop listening because they have obviously heard it before.

It is worth writing a new and different Close for this second Close. The people who have remained will be Closed twice. You will have asked them in two different ways to do what you want them to do. There is nothing wrong with that.

"What if I expect questions and get none?"

Typically you begin the Q & A session with, "Before I CLOSE, what questions do you have?" Wait silently for the count of 10 (count to 5 on the telephone).

If there are no questions and you know there should be some, there are ways to encourage them:

- "A question I frequently get is…" Say one of the questions and answers you have anticipated. When finished say, "What is the next question?"

- A humorous way to handle a quiet group is to ask, "What is the first question?" Wait. If there is no response say, "What is the second question?" Wait for the laughter to stop. Usually a question comes. If not, use, "A question I frequently get is…"

- You can point to your watch and say, "Let me give you a minute to turn to the people near you and come up with some questions." Although people may be hesitant to speak in front of the larger group, they will readily interact with those around them. After a minute say, "Please finish up." Wait 15 seconds for them to stop. You may have to repeat, "Please come back." Wait for complete silence before starting again.

- Ask each of the groups for one question and continue around the room asking for one question. Respond to each immediately or write down all the questions in categories but do not answer them. After you have collected all of the questions, you decide the order in which to reply or choose the questions you want to answer.

- Do not take all the questions from the first group and move on group by group - by the time you get to the last group, their questions may have already been asked and they may think, "Why did we have to work so hard to come up with questions?"

When you have handled all of the questions, say,

"LET ME LEAVE YOU WITH THIS..." and Close.

"Should I have a friend ask the first question?"

Unfortunately, this technique often does not work. Either the person forgets to ask, or says, "She told me to ask this question."

"I run out of time. I can't answer all the questions because I need to Close."

- Since Rule #2 is End on Time, keep an eye on the time and stop the Q & A a few minutes early.
- Say, "I want to Close, but I will stay after to answer the remaining questions" or "I want to Close, but I invite you to email me your remaining questions."

"I don't know an answer. I should / should not know it."

If you *should* know the answer

If you do not have information you should know, apologize and offer to get it for them. Say,

"I should have that information for you. If you would like, at the next break, I will get it."

Or "I will get you that information as soon as I get back to my office." Ask someone in the group, "May I send it to you to broadcast to everyone?"

Since you have made a promise, your credibility is on the line. Get them the information immediately.

If you *should not* know the answer

Say,

> "I will get that information for you from the expert in my company. I will send it to you."

Do not tell them the name of the expert, because that person may be peeved that you directed calls to him, unless it is company policy.

Your request is more of a priority to you than to the expert. Say,

> "I know that you are busy. This is so important to the client/meeting, would you get me that information as quickly as you can?" Be sure to thank the expert and let others in the company know how you were helped.

"Someone gives a speech instead of asking a question!"

These people raise hands as if to ask a question. Instead of asking, they give a speech to show everyone how smart they are. These people do this regularly, not just to you!

In addition to *you* not being allowed to waste the listeners' time, you can't allow *someone else* to waste their time. First the group is angry at the talker and then they get angry at you because you are allowing the person to waste their time.

You would think others would stop the non-stop talker, wouldn't you? They won't. They look to you to stop the talker.

Although you may wish you didn't have to gently confront the person, you must.

Here are various techniques. Try one - if it doesn't work, try another. (You know that the exception to this is if the talker is your Boss or another important person.)

1. As soon as you realize you have a talker, wait for him/her to inhale and then interrupt. You must interrupt because they won't stop talking! Ask, "Do you have a question?" with an expectant look on your face. This alerts the person that you know what he is doing and may make him stop. He may say, "I really don't have a question but I just wanted to say..." and then stop.

2. If he continues wasting others' time, do what the politicians do. After the talker says something positive, interrupt with, "It is interesting you should say that ..." and talk about that subject to get the attention back on you. Break eye contact with that person as soon as you deliver this and do not return your eyes to him.

3. Is he is still talking? Interrupt with, "I would like to hear this but I must take more questions/finish my material/move on. Could we meet after? I will stay here after my talk/the meeting and those of you who want to can join us." Be careful to speak in a neutral tone since it is very easy to use hostile, sarcastic tones with this person.

4. Finally, if he will not stop, break eye contact and look at the other participants. Interrupt the speaker and ask the others, "Would it be okay with you if he and I meet after this to continue?"

   a. Sometimes they say, "Oh no, we want to hear it." In that case, let him finish. You do not need to answer because there has been no question. Say,

"Thank you. Who else has a question?" as you look at another quadrant in the room.

b. Usually, however, all the people who have been quiet up until now will suddenly join in a chorus of, "Yes, great idea, let's move on." Look around the room and call on the next person.

"I made a mistake in my answer."

When you realize you made a mistake, say in a neutral voice,

"I made a mistake about the _____. It really is....."

Everyone makes mistakes - by appearing confident, you indicate that your material is good and this was simply a misstep.

You set the emotional tone of the room as the speaker - looking upset and uncomfortable causes an empathetic audience to feel upset and uncomfortable with you. Or, a predator in the audience may attack.

"My Boss Answers for me!"

Reasonable and Unreasonable Bosses

If the Boss is a Reasonable Person

See the boss privately. Use this template to structure your conversation:

1. Agree to meet for a specified amount of time
   - Begin with, "Is this a good time to talk without interruption?"

- By getting a yes, the person will less likely attempt to escape with, "I just remembered I have to call someone" when you say something that makes him/her feel uncomfortable.

2. "May I say a few things first and then can we have a discussion?"

Getting this agreement will enable you to stop any interruptions during the first part by saying, "I just have a bit more to say, and then I'd like us to have a discussion. Would that be okay?"

3. Positive Intent

There is *some* positive reason the person does the behavior that you do not like.

"Helen, (the Boss), I appreciate that you want people to leave the meeting with accurate information."

4. Say how You Perceive It

"You may not realize it but when I don't get to answer, people may think I don't know the information. I noticed that they started directing their questions to you. Since I am the key contact for this group, I want them to have confidence that I am qualified to help them."

5. Your Proposal

"How about, for the next three meetings, I answer each question and then end with, 'Helen would you like to add something?' That way they will know I am the primary contact and I sincerely want them to get complete information."

"Or, I can handle the answers completely, and you and I can meet afterward so you can tell me what you would have said."

6. Get Input

"Can we work something out here? What do you think?"

Listen and negotiate an agreement.

Often a reasonable boss will say, "I had no idea that my answering might be taken that way. I do not want to undermine your standing with the client. Sure, let's try this."

If the Boss is an Unreasonable Person

You will usually not get a micro-manager to change behavior. Try to retain your credibility and dignity by starting a client conversation with,

"I will give you my ideas and then I'd like to ask Helen (the boss) if she would like to add to that."
Be sure to use a neutral voice.

Do not allow yourself to get upset about something over which you have no control.

"Should I repeat the question?"

- If you feel that some people have not heard the question, repeat it. If everyone has heard the question, don't repeat it.
- In a large group, have someone in the front row remind you to repeat a question if it was said quietly.
- If the question is unclear, repeat what you heard so the person asking has a chance to clarify.

- If the question is an attack, rephrase it positively for the group. For example, "The new software is terrible. What are you going to do about it?" becomes, "What improvements would you like us to make in the new software?"

"The question is irrelevant."

Respond with, "That would be good to address, but we need to cover today's agenda. How about we...

- ...put that on the agenda for Wednesday's meeting?"
- ...form a small group to come up with recommendations?"
- ...discuss that at the end of the meeting?"
- ...put it on the board to discuss later?"

You may decide if it would be best to answer this irrelevant question. For example, if the person asking this question signs your paycheck or has some power to hurt your career, you may want to briefly answer.

"She is asking for a consultation right now."

Avoid the temptation to help someone at length during the talk. Unless it this is relevant to the entire group, you break Rule #1, Don't waste my time.

To continue on with your presentation, say,

> "I want to help you with that. Can we set up a time for us to talk and get into that in depth? Would you meet with me after this to set up an appointment? My purpose today is just the overview of the project."

You can also ask the group if they prefer you handle it now or connect with this person later.

"The question is vague or unclear."

After hearing the question, paraphrase (say what you heard).

After you paraphrase, the person will either say, "Yes, that that is what I meant" or they will clarify.

It is important to appear to be polite by keeping your voice neutral. The rest of the group is watching your behavior in this challenging situation and will judge you poorly if you show impatience or use sarcasm.

"I can't understand the accent."

Re-state what you heard and ask for confirmation. Repeat this until you really do understand the question.

When people see how sincerely you honor the questioner and want to understand, they will jump into the conversation to help you. They may be co-workers of the questioner. Don't sound condescending or exasperated.

"I just answered a question but she was looking at her phone and asked the same question."

or

"The person asked a stupid question."

All of the eyes in the room are watching to see your reaction and your response! Do not embarrass the person. Keep your dignity and respect theirs.

Look the questioner in the eye, and using a neutral voice, answer the question. End with, "Does that answer your question?" After the person says, "Yes," look at another quadrant of the room. Ask, "Who has the next question?"

Do not say, "As I said before." Or, "If you had been listening…" It is better to win the respect that comes by taking the "high road" and being considerate.

You show everyone they can trust you and you will not embarrass them when they make mistakes.

"They are asking for information I am not allowed to reveal."

With clients:

> "I am sure you understand I am not allowed to reveal that information."

With employees:

People hear rumors and want honest information about their futures. Bosses make a mistake when they deny having information. It is best to say the truth,

> "I know that information but I am not allowed to reveal it yet. As soon as I can, I will tell you immediately."

CHAPTER 9

Time Management as you Speak

Obviously, the only way to determine how long your talk will be is to rehearse it aloud and time it. Reading it or mumbling it does not give an accurate measurement.

You can rehearse pieces and segments of a talk and time each one.

Often your time will be cut short. Indicate on your notes what you will leave out should that happen. Time your delivery of this this abbreviated talk.

During the talk, place a watch or clock next to your notes. End on time.

"Fear makes me Speed Up."

Many people speak faster when nervous. Rehearse the first five minutes of your talk speaking very slowly. This helps you develop the habit of slow pacing.

"I must speak fast to get in all of my information."

People do not receive or retain information when the speaker presents it too quickly. Deliver edited material to give yourself time to speak slowly.

"My time was cut short!"

Any interruption, either a question or unexpected event, steals your time. For example, the speakers before you exceed their time limits or an important person joins the meeting and asks to "Say a few words." Or, the afternoon snack arrives (You will soon see it is advantageous not to stand between people and food). Therefore:

Edit While Speaking

For example:

Joe Theismann, a popular American football player, was the opening keynote speaker for a weekend of meetings. He was scheduled to speak for 45 minutes.

Before Theismann came up, the event coordinator thanked those who participated in the planning of the event and explained which buildings would be used for lunch and for the various seminars. Someone else presented awards and allowed recipients to give short thank you talks.

Finally it was time for Joe Theismann to speak. There were 22 minutes left.

He was a good speaker; motivating, inspiring and funny. He was finished in 22 minutes and ended at the scheduled time.

How did Theismann do it?

First, this is what he did *not* do:

- He did not speak fast to squeeze his planned 45 minutes of information into 22 minutes.
- He did not say, "Oh, I am so sorry our time was cut short. I had so many more stories to tell you." He did not make people feel as if they missed anything.

What he did:

- Theismann delivered his talk with confidence because before he even arrived, he had chosen the parts he would leave out if his time were cut short.

Pre-edit

- Some people write a 45-minute talk to go with their visuals. They also write a 30-minute talk and a 20-minute talk for the same visuals. They are prepared to switch notes when their time is shortened.

"But if listeners are looking at screens or if they have the handout, how can I leave anything out?"

- Since they do not know what you intended to say about each idea, you can confidently deliver the edited version.
- For example, if there are three bullets on a page and you now want to speak about only the first two - after the second bullet, put up the third bullet but say only a summary sentence instead of your entire planned piece. Although you had planned to speak fully about

all three bullets, the listeners do not know that. They do not have your notes.

- Although you had expected to give information in the talk and even had a visual with the information, skip the visual and unapologetically tell them how they will receive it.
- By anticipating and preparing for your time to be cut short, you will feel more at ease.

Editing as a Participant on a Panel

For example:

I observed a panel with five participants. The first four speakers went over their allotted time because the facilitator did not cut them off. (When you are the facilitator, please enforce time designations.)

The last speaker had three minutes left. He said, "I have three minutes. I will give you the most important take-away ideas." And he did.

He was the most memorable speaker of the day.

CHAPTER 10

Visuals Attract Attention & Make You Memorable

www.glasbergen.com

"Any chance you could learn PowerPoint
before your next presentation, Jim?"

The Right Reasons to Use Visuals

Most people learn best with visual stimulation (the other inputs are auditory and kinesthetic). Adding visuals to your talk can make you a more powerful presenter.

- Words and ideas will be better understood when people see them on a bulleted list as well as hear them.
- You can increase comprehension with a graphic or chart.
- Visuals make the entire presentation more memorable.

The Wrong Reasons to use Visuals

You will not make a positive impact if your motivations are:

- "I want people to look at the visuals and pay less attention to me."
- "I want to read the visuals to them so I don't really have to give a speech."
- "I use them because my boss said I must."

You *do not* have to use PowerPoint

Analyze the group and the situation. If everyone else uses a white board or flip charts or handouts, either do the same to fit in or choose to be different. If being different will distract them, use what everyone else uses.

How to Add Visuals to your Presentation

- Write your talk first!
- Do not write whole sentences on the screen. When you write your entire talk on the screen, they think,

    "I can read the talk. I don't need you to read it to me. Email it."

- Instead, put an outline on the screen. *You deliver the complete ideas to fill in the outline.* (Note: When you must send your talk to those who did not attend, write the whole talk and send it to them.)
- If it will help the group, include Agenda/Preview Summary and/or Review Summary screens.
- What points are best explained with a chart, a table, or a photograph? Make it easy to grasp the ideas.
- Use your organization's template and your boss's preferences if required.

> **TIP**
> Rehearse with your visuals.
> Become comfortable with the "choreography"
> of clicking, pausing and speaking.

Delivering "Company-Prepared" Screens

Some visuals prepared by the company can have problems:

- Some fonts are too small to read, especially on charts. Read the material aloud using your laptop for reference, still facing the listeners.
- If there are too many screens to address in the time allotted, you might edit and say, "Let me show you the highlights" and describe only those. Or say, "The main idea of this screen is..." and skip less important points.
- Make your talk interesting by adding Supports.

Avoid Mistakes with Visuals

Do not read the screens to them

- People will read each screen as soon as it is shown, even before you begin to talk. Use some of the same words from the screen as you elaborate.
- You are doubly ruined if you turn your back to listeners to face the screen while you read to them.

Who can hold people's attention while turning their back to the listeners? No one.

Do not squeeze too much material one screen

If you have many bullets, duplicate the heading on two or three screens and divide the bullets among them.

Do not use flashy, blinking, exciting visuals or sounds

Some in the group will stop listening to you and think, "I like how that looks! I'd like to learn that. Maybe my kid can show me."

How many screens to use?

Use the number of screens that will help your listeners to learn. It could be any number.

Layout and Appearance of Screens

© Randy Glasbergen
www.glasbergen.com

GLASBERGEN

"Because a large font makes profits look bigger."

- Leave the bottom third blank.
- Have more white space than print.
- Limit yourself to two or three fonts/page.
- Make fonts large enough so the person farthest away can easily see.

- Use color, because it helps people remember ideas more easily.

As You Deliver your Talk

- Be silent as they read each new screen.
- As they look at each screen, glance at your laptop or printed notes laying on the table. Look up and resume speaking.
- Stand close to the table to easily see your notes. Do not do a dance of standing centrally, stepping over to see notes & returning to center.
- If you hold printed notes - train yourself to look at your filled-in outline in one hand and then put that arm down at your side. Gesture with the other hand to avoid waving your notes.
- Webinar/Teleseminar - Put your notes on a flip chart posted behind the camera. You can easily glance between them and the camera.
- Use words to direct their attention to certain parts of the screen such as, "Look at the top line on the graph." There is no need to gesture toward the screen.

If Someone Else will Change your Screens

Rehearse with the person. Give them your notes with screen-change notations.

If the Boss Won't Let You use Notes

Rehearse repeatedly with notes so that just looking at each bullet on the screen will cue your thinking. Memorize the Opener and Close.

If you must use the screen for your cues:

1. Stop talking
2. Look at the screen
3. Turn to the listeners
4. Begin speaking again

Use Less Laser Pointing

There is little reason to point to the screen with a laser pointer. When you say, "Look at the second bullet," they will look at it.

Use words to direct their attention. Examples:

- "Look at the third bar on the graph. That is fourth quarter of last year. Compare it to the last bar on the right…"
- "Look at the top of the chart."
- "Look at the top line of this graph, the blue one with the dots on it." Some people are color blind - in addition to color, add and refer to dots or dashes on the screen.

If you must use a Laser Pointer

1. Stop talking
2. Turn
3. Hold your arm against your body to minimize shaking the laser pointer
4. Circle the item slowly
5. Turn back to the listeners
6. Begin speaking again

> **TIP**
>
> Memorize the feel of the buttons so you do not need to look at the clicker. Do not shake your hand as you press.

Prior to showing a Complicated Visual

- If you are showing the "big picture" on a chart, introduce it by saying, "First, let me show you a screen with all of the information on it. Then I will highlight different elements."
- Just like a printed map, you can place a box around a part of the chart or graph. Enlarge that segment on the next screen and talk about it. The following screen can be a repeat of the big picture.

Using PowerPoint

- Use a wireless clicker to change the screens. If your company will not buy one for you, buy and carry your own. You want to look good.
- You can make the screen go black so that all of the attention is on you for a story or a strong statement. On the keyboard, press "B." To have the PowerPoint screen return, press "B" again. To make the screen go white, press "W." To have the screen return, press "'W" again.
- When you speak offsite, especially out of the country, email your PowerPoint presentation to yourself and a contact person. Also, copy it to a memory stick. These

backups help if your laptop does not work or if items get lost.

- In addition, print your presentation with three screens on a page and bring this printed (hard) copy with you. If the projection system fails, you can ask for this to be copied for the participants. Announce, "The system is down. No problem. While we are having the presentation copied, let me tell you what the next screen will say so we can keep working." Assure them that although this issue has occurred, their time will not be wasted.

"I have the results of your brain scan. We found evidence of extensive PowerPoint damage."

Flip Charts

Prepare charts in advance and write the name of each on one corner that you have bent forward. Flip your charts to the back of the easel and pull them to front as needed.

- Leave the bottom third blank.
- Have more white space than writing.
- Write legibly. Use print that is easier to read than your usual handwriting.
- Write large enough so the person farthest away can easily see.
- Color helps people to more easily remember ideas. Avoid yellow and orange - too difficult to see.
- Write your own notes in pencil on the flip chart. No one will see them and you will look very smart.
- When you are finished with a topic, flip to the next page or a blank page.

Handouts

Handouts are a nightmare - people read them when you want them to be watching and listening to you. They skip to the back and ruin your buildup to a big finish.

However, you can be successful using handouts. Have the handouts already at people's places so they can flip through them before you begin.

Since you are now competing with your handout for their attention:

Capture their attention with a great Opener. You must overcome their desire to continue looking at the handout.

- Then say, "Please turn to page 2. Page 2." Wait until most people have turned to the proper page; not everyone will follow your instruction. Begin speaking.
- If you skip a page, explain why. "This next page is a review of the previous material. Please turn to page 18." Or, if you skip a page because you have run out of time, "This next page explains the new template. I will email this to you."
- Force yourself to not be distracted by those people who continue to read the handout while you are speaking. Some people will never look at you. Speak to those who are paying attention.

  When you need someone's attention, say the person's name before you begin giving the important information, "Jean, this is the information I wanted you to see." The person will look up from the handout and pay attention to you.

Handouts at a Convention

- Print 50% more than you need since people who will not attend your session may pick yours up on the way to another's lecture.
- Have them on people's seats before the session. Ask others to do this for you.
- Be sure your contact information is on the handout.

Distributing a handout during the session invites chaos. Either have it available before the talk or deliver it at the door as people leave.

Showing Products

Hold the product still as you speak. Pass it around for inspection during the break or after the program. If you pass it while you speak, the person looking at it will not listen to you and everyone else will be watching the person looking at it.

CHAPTER 11

Keep your Accent but make it Charming

How can you make sure *everyone* understands you, even the first time you speak?

These guidelines avoid the common mistakes made by people who speak English as a second language:

- Clearly pronounce each sound of each word, especially the final sound. It is tempting to blur words together; don't do it.

- Speak slowly enough. It is difficult to understand even native speakers when they speak too quickly. Hint: When you feel you are speaking *too slowly*, you are probably using the correct speed. Ask a colleague for feedback.

- Speak loud enough. When people ask you to speak louder, it is often not your accent that they are referring to. They really just can't hear you. When you think you are speaking *too loudly*, you are probably using the right volume. Ask for feedback.

- Imagine yourself as an actor playing the part of an American giving a speech. An actor can be comfortable using a speaking style that is not his own.

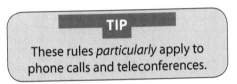

TIP

These rules *particularly* apply to phone calls and teleconferences.

Addressing New People

When speaking to new people, some of them may think, "I wonder where she's from." While they are thinking about your country of origin, *they are not listening to you!*

Why do they have these questions? The most primitive part of our brains still categorizes others as safe, belonging to our tribe, helpful, etc.

You can't control their thinking - but you may be able to direct it

After your Opener, you may want to reference your background. Be sure it relates to your talk.

Examples:

- "When I was a kid growing up in Honduras, (tell a story that makes the point of your talk)."

- "My uncle in India used to give me advice when I was a child." Say the quotation and perhaps add, "There is a similar saying here in the U.S. It is _____."
- "In old China... (tell a *brief* folk tale)"
- "In Kentucky, we used to say, _____."

You have revealed a little about yourself and put an emphasis on your main idea in an interesting way. At the same time, you bring their attention back to your content.

Who uses a similar technique?

Watch a standup comedian. If there is *anything* that may cause people to focus on something other than what he is saying (For example: he looks like a famous person or is very tall or short), the first joke addresses the issue and consequently dismisses it. Use your history to your advantage.

"I can't remember the word in English."

- Rehearse talks aloud using user-friendly outline notes. When you remember the word, add it to your notes as a reminder during the actual talk.
- While speaking, it is fine to ask, "What is the word that means (explain the meaning)?"

"I do not like to ask for definitions of unfamiliar words."

You are lucky because you have a lifetime "honeymoon" of permission to ask the definition of any word or phrase or ask for the explanation of a joke.

> Say, "I learned English as a second language. What does that mean?"

Each time, feel pride that you are able to move between different cultures and languages while functioning well in both. It is enviable.

"My Boss complains that my Email does not contain correct English."

Create your material in a Microsoft Word type of program with an auto correction feature. Cut and paste it into email. The only way to improve is to ask someone to look over your email before sending it. Study the suggestions given and use them next time. *Writing with mistakes could hold you back in your career.*

Learn Relevant Words and Improve Grammar

Instead of learning random words from a vocabulary book, each day listen for a word or grammatical rule that you do not yet use.

Also, ask a friend to correct your pronunciation and grammar.

> For example: "Michele, at the meeting today I would like you to notice any words I could pronounce better, or some grammar that I could improve. Would you do that? You can tell me after the meeting."

> She will say yes, but at the end of the meeting she may say she didn't hear anything. This could be because she is familiar with your delivery or is uncomfortable correcting you.

Assure her, "I know I speak English well but I want to polish my language skills. You are helping me to grow professionally, not criticizing me. I would really appreciate your help."

Ask before and after several meetings until she feels comfortable giving you feedback.

What to do with a suggestion? Use it three times during the remainder of the day or the next day to memmorize it.

Suggestions: make yourself think in English instead of translating. Read books and watch films in English.

"I hesitate to speak in meetings."

You may think, "I am a subordinate and should not speak up," "I'm shy," "I don't want to say something wrong."

But your *colleagues may* think, "You don't want to help," "You keep your good ideas to yourself."

Notice that not everything your colleagues say is brilliant, yet they continue to share their ideas. Colleagues forgive each other's suggestions and ideas that are not "perfect."

Although it may be difficult to change your behavior with elders and authority, it can be done. Be one of the first to speak at meetings to minimize fear build-up and indicate you want to contribute.

"I want to feel part of this culture."

Spend more social time with native English speakers. Ask them to give you an orientation to their favorite things. Invite them to your home and they will reciprocate.

"I never understand the jokes."

It is appropriate to ask someone at the time, or afterward, to explain the joke. People may find you delightful if you then use the joke appropriately.

Many jokes reference cultural experiences the native speakers were exposed to as children such as television shows, books and movies.

It is never too late to have these social experiences. Read the books and see the films your colleagues have enjoyed. A French client told me he heard the phrase, "Ignore the man behind the curtain" for seven years but did not understand it until he saw the film, "The Wizard of Oz."

CHAPTER 12

More Speaking Opportunities

Addressing Bosses and Boards

Be Brief

- Bosses and Board Members usually prefer hearing results and recommendations. They usually trust you, as the expert, have done the research and work required.

- Be concise while focusing on the main ideas of your talk. Give details when asked.

- Add visuals if they will help listeners to understand your ideas.

Prepare

- Don't think because you work well under pressure you should be spontaneous and "wing it." You may be good but you won't be great.

- Rehearse aloud by yourself or with colleagues.
- *Expect questions* about the niche of each attendee and practice the answers aloud. Ask colleagues how to handle the difficult people who may be present.
- Minimize day-of-the-talk stress - the night before, ready your materials.
- Stay focused. Read through the stress management and "self-talk" suggestions in this book.

Video Conferences, Teleconferences & Webinars

"Hair stylist, makeup artist, body double, stunt coordinator, best boy, gaffer, dolly grip... Will this be your first video conference?"

Video Conference Call

- Rehearse in front of a mirror to become aware of distracting behaviors.
- Rehearse and rehearse again.
- Look into the camera 80% of the time, even if you have listeners in the room with you.
- Do not wear clothing with patterns that will appear to vibrate on the screen.

Teleconference and Webinar

Your voice is the only tool you have to create a professional impression on each teleconference and webinar.

Almost everyone sounds more authoritative when they begin speaking slowly with precise articulation. Be sure to pre-choose Voice Variety and note it on your notes.

Hold Their Attention

What you can do

- Alert people that you will be asking for responses when you have finished delivering your ideas. Say their names *before* you give the information. For example, "Herb, Lin and Jose, this is the information you were looking for. I would like each of you to make a comment when I finish."
- Ask questions to check-in and gauge the participants' comprehension. "Are you following me?" "Would you like me to clarify any part of this?" "What questions do you have so far?" *Don't use the same question repeatedly.* Adjust your talk based on their feedback.

- Capture attention, also, by asking for individual responses.

  For example,
  - "Joe and Jane, is this what you had in mind?" Wait for them to contribute.
  - "Bob, can you see where we are going here?"
- Keep in mind that certain colleagues or customers around the globe may not respond to questions when their bosses are on the call! Accept their behavior as part of doing business with them. Connect after the call to get what you need.

Facilitating a Conference Call or Teleseminar

- Although you may be the leader of the team or project, you do not have to be the facilitator or moderator of a conference call or teleseminar. Ask someone with those skills to lead, or rotate the role among participants.
- Before the meeting, send out the Agenda with names of who will be presenting each issue. It encourages people to come prepared and to anticipate questions they may receive.
- When the meeting goes off on a tangent, make a decision if this addition is appropriate to delve into at this time. If it is not, the leader can say, "That is an important issue to discuss. I will schedule it to be addressed later. Let's continue with the agenda for this meeting."

Webinar Technology

- If you will be taking questions through web conference software, text or email, schedule a break in which to respond. You could have someone assist you by reading and deciding which should be forwarded to you for discussion.

- Use polls only when they add to the material. Everyone resents being asked to participate in a poll when the goal is not for information gathering but to manipulate participants to engage.

At the Close of the Meeting

As in all meetings, the leader should summarize what all are to do after the meeting, i.e. "Next Steps"

- Who will do it?
- What will be accomplished?
- By which dates and times?

Group Delivery

"If we want to succeed as a team, we need to put aside our own selfish, individual interests and start doing things my way."

- As others speak, look at them as though you are listening.

- Do not distract from others' talks: prepare and reorganize your materials before and after the program, not when others are presenting.

- Rehearse the transitions. How will you pass the microphone? Will you stand or sit? How long will each person speak? Will you have some "please finish" alert system?

- For important meetings, rehearse the entire program to be sure you are not missing or repeating information.

- Decide ahead when you will take questions. This is the speakers' choice – take them as you speak or wait until the end. Announce your preference *after the Opener*:

    For example: "My name is Ina Gerson. Today I will introduce the program. Muriel will go next to explain the logistics, and Leonard will close with the plan moving forward. Please hold questions until the end and direct them to any of the speakers."

    Or, "...and Leonard will close with the plan moving forward. Please ask any questions as we go along. If a question will be answered later in our program, we may hold off answering it until we reach that point."

Panels

When you are a Speaker on the Panel

Before the event, call the meeting planner or contact person to get information for your preparation. Email is not as reliable as telephoning. People will usually write brief answers without the subtleties you would uncover in a call. As a consequence, you may prepare too much, too little or even the wrong material.

Ask the contact person:

- How many other speakers will present?
- What are the topics of the other speakers?
- Who will go first, second, etc.?
- How much time does each person have?
- How much depth should I go into?
- What time of day will I be speaking? (Add more Supports if you are speaking in the afternoon.)

"I think the Other Panelist is Wrong."

Do not argue with other speakers. When you disagree, show respect by speaking with a neutral tone of voice as you say,

- "There are many points of view on this issue. I will tell you mine and explain why I feel it is valid."
- "I look at it this way."
- "What I've learned..."

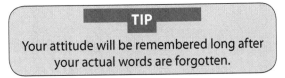

TIP

Your attitude will be remembered long after your actual words are forgotten.

When You are the Facilitator of the Panel

As soon as the panel is announced, alert each of the speakers about:

- The theme and purpose of the panel
- The identities and topics of the other speakers
- The time allotted to each person

Let them know that there will be someone timing them who will say softly (or hold up a sign), "Five minutes left," "One minute left," and, "Thank you." Let them know you will enforce the time allotment. Do this to be fair, to end on time, and to keep the audience's respect.

Pre-program Logistics

Call the venue and get the names and phone numbers of the audio visual (A/V) specialists and room-set-up people. You may need them.

Regardless of how clearly your written, confirmed instructions are, the room, microphones and A/V are often not set up as requested on the day of the meeting. Do not get angry or start blaming others - people tend to be more helpful when you act civilly. Arrive earlier than you think you need to and check that all microphones, visuals and recording devices are working.

Ask the Speakers to send you their Introductions

- Ask them for a few sentences that indicate why they are appropriate to be on this panel.
- This is not the time to use their life's biography or curriculum vitae. Print their more extensive descriptions of them in the handout.

Prepare your Opener and Close

The Opener

Do not make the mistake of delivering a very long Opener. Prepare no more than a short paragraph introducing the topic and each presenter; then let the panelists do their jobs.

The Close

You must prepare something to bring the program to an end. It is not enough to say, "Well, thank you all for coming."

You might say, "Our purpose here today was to explore/ update/introduce _____ *(the topic)* ___. Thank you, Panelists, for your contributions."

Logistics of the Panel

- Tell speakers that they do not have to lean in to any microphone. The mikes are sensitive enough to capture their voices.

- Ask them to not distract when others are speaking. For example: shuffling papers, speaking to one another or acknowledging people in the room. Although this sounds basic, many people do not consider the impact these actions have on listeners.

Speak to Large Groups

"If I can get abducted by aliens this morning, I won't have to give my presentation this afternoon!"

Preparation

- Prior to your presentation, pretend you are giving, "an important speech" when talking at regular meetings. That is, prepare for each with notes and rehearsal just as you will in an important talk.

- If the large group meeting will allow for questions, prepare for the toughest ones you may receive. Ask your boss, the legal department and others to coach you on appropriate responses.

- Go to the meeting room early. Stand where you will stand and imagine you are successfully helping the listeners. See them appreciating what you are saying.

- Arrange to rehearse with A/V support people prior to the meeting, even if for a few minutes.

- If anything can't be done the way you want, adjust and do the best you can. Never announce the difficulties to the audience.

Delivery

- Speak as you normally speak, using a conversational style. Speaking more formally will lose the listeners' interest.

- Although you may not see their eyes well, address the four quadrants of the room so all members of the audience feel you are directing some attention towards them.

- Do not turn to the screen and read the visual. If you must use the screen as your notes, turn in silence as you read a new screen, then turn back to speak to the group.

- Rarely use a laser pointer. Use your words to direct their attention to different parts of the screen. If you must use a laser pointer, face the screen in silence and make slow circles on the point of interest. Turn back to people and speak.

Avoid Making Yourself Crazy

Do not allow your mind to wander with thoughts such as, "I'm speaking to such a huge group!" If that is your habit, force yourself to look at and speak to only one or two people at a time. Speak to them conversationally as you always do. Work this way around the quadrants of the room.

Introductions

You are being Introduced

- Send the person introducing you a one paragraph bio with the facts that are relevant to this the audience. Double-space the document and provide phonetic spellings for words or names, if helpful.
- Although you have sent your introduction before the program, still bring a copy with you in case the introducer forgets to bring it.
- Smile and look at the speaker as you are being introduced.
- Wait until the introduction is finished before walking on the platform. Begin speaking after you have settled into place.
- Stand still and slowly deliver your Opener with eye contact and voice strength. Glance at printed notes or

the laptop during the Body of the talk. Try for 100% eye contact while delivering the Close.

You Introducing Others

When you receive the speaker's introduction, shorten it and print it double spaced for easy reading. Say it aloud, ahead of time, to identify words that require pronunciation help.

After delivering the introduction, wait until the guest is about to arrive on stage before you leave your spot. Sit down without drawing attention to yourself.

Toasts

Think of positive experiences that indicate the personality and character the honoree. Practice and bring notes. Stick to what you planned to say. Don't drink alcohol before your talk.

Using Humor

Try your material on someone before the event. Value their opinion as to whether this material is appropriate to use for this person, this group and this occasion.

The Roast-Toast

This is where you tell listeners about embarrassing behaviors or experiences the honoree has had. People will remember you instead of the honoree if your toast is in bad taste - stick to what you planned to say instead of being spontaneous. Definitely hold off on drinking alcohol until *after* your talk.

After Lunch/After Dinner Speech

It is an honor and privilege to be invited to speak after a meal. *It is a career opportunity to be so visible.*

Accept the *after-lunch* talk invitation - people are usually receptive.

Decline the *after-dinner* speech invitation - people are usually tired and sometimes drunk. If you must accept it, be succinct, be humorous and get off the platform.

- In an after-meal talk, every word counts. You will usually speak for 45 minutes.
- Rehearse, rehearse, and rehearse.
- In rehearsal, when you make mistakes, correct them and keep speaking just as you will do when you make errors in the real talk. You *will* make mistakes; practice appearing unconcerned.
- Since you are competing with food, you must use your most leadership-sounding voice to get and hold their attention. Appear confident, especially in the first five minutes, regardless of how you actually feel.

> **TIP**
> Arrange to have the wait staff to stop serving and removing dishes while you speak.

- Be sure to have an engaging Opener and a compelling Close for the talk. Use Supports - stories, examples and unusual ideas and say them with Voice Variety. Entertain as you educate.

- After you have prepared your talk, decide if a handout or PowerPoint would be helpful. Have the handout and your business card at each plate when they arrive.
- Give your contact information in the Body of the talk so that your Close will leave them with an action step. Pause when you finish and accept their applause.

Business Networking

Many people make good contacts at local meetings of professional organizations and at national/international conventions.

Accept that it is normal to be a little apprehensive about meeting new people. You will sound smart and qualified when you do what you have learned in this book.

- When meeting new people, be interested in their work before you speak about your business. Building the relationship is more important than pitching your product and service.
- Listen carefully to other people's challenges and commiserate. If you can help solve their problems, ask if they would like to hear your ideas.
- Have a goal. For example, for them simply to know your business exists or to set an appointment.

> **TIP**
>
> Emphasize how you can solve their specific issues, not all that your organization offers.

BONUS

Cope with Difficult People & Difficult Situations

There are challenging people in almost every workplace. Some are openly hostile, some sabotage, etc.

Guidelines

- Before meetings or telephone calls, ask others who know the particiipants what each person might say or ask about your ideas and materials. Prepare and rehearse your responses aloud.

- When attacked by a predator, it is human behavior to cower and be quiet. Appear confident when you are in a stressful situation by using the same voice, eye contact and gestures you have used already in the meeting.

- Outside of a meeting, find ways to positively acknowledge and make the difficult peoples' jobs and lives easier. Perhaps they will target a different person next time.

Ask yourself, "Does this person do this to everyone or just to me?"

- If you are one of the few who is bothered by this person, examine what you are doing that may contribute to the situation. Are you passive? Do you not defend your boundaries? These behaviors may invite an aggressive person to attack. Are you so reactive that it is entertaining to the person to set you off on an emotional tangent?
- Identify other people who are not victims of the difficult person. Ask them to mentor you on the wording and delivery of new messages and behaviors to use in future interactions.

Difficult Participant Behaviors

Someone takes Credit for Your Work

- Make sure others, especially higher management, know what work you have done. Do this by casually talking about projects you are working on and have completed. For example:

  When someone asks, "How are you doing?" respond with how excited you are about the project you are working on, giving details.

The Person who Repeats the Same Points

When you are the speaker/leader, you facilitate the conversation. Some people repeat their points several times during one statement; they can't believe everyone has understood the idea so they re-state it. This repetition wastes the group's time so you must interrupt.

Summarize what he/she said to assure that you have received it. Then lead the conversation to the next point.

The Non-Stop Talker

- In casual conversation with peers or staff, interrupt with,

    "That reminds me of..." and begin to go off on your own tangent. Be sure to break eye contact with the non-stop talker and speak to others.

- Or look at a different person and say her name, "Jane, didn't a similar thing happen to you?" to focus the spotlight on someone else.

- When speaking one-to-one with the non-stop talker, say you must get back to work. Stop responding and either leave or walk the person into someone else's office.

The Latecomer to the Meeting

- If the people already in the meeting stop listening to watch the latecomer get seated, stop talking. Be silent until he/she is almost settled and then repeat your last idea to get listener attention back on you.

- If the latecomer slips in unnoticed, there is no need to stop.

Should I review the material for the latecomer?

Consider the importance and influence of the person walking in late.

If it is an important person or someone critical to the discussion, give a 15 second re-cap of what you have already covered.

If the person does not fall into either of these categories, continue with your talk.

The Person who Speaks Louder than you and Takes Away Listeners' Attention

Someone "talking over you" usually is a result you speaking too quietly.

To take back the listeners' attention, say in a louder voice, "I would like to finish what I was saying" and continue speaking. Obviously, consider how the person and the participants might react to this before taking this step.

> **TIP**
>
> Give over the spotlight to certain people, such as the person who signs your paycheck.

The Person criticizes you Personally as well as Professionally

Manipulative people will criticize you personally along with disapproval of your work. Use constructive solutions rather than attempting to say equally negative remarks.

Saboteurs try to invalidate and discredit people. They try
to make you uncomfortable so that they look good by
comparison. They will wait until you are in front of others to
ask you a question they know you do not know.

© Randy Glasbergen
glasbergen.com

"I have a note from my doctor. I'm allergic to criticism!"

- Stay calm. People will remember you stayed cool while
  dealing with this hostile behavior.

- Speak only about work issues, events, behaviors and
  what was said or done, but not personalities. Ignore
  personal attacks. Respond by asking about what was,
  or needs to be, said or done.

- Ask questions. If the criticism is general or vague such
  as, "Is your work always this incomplete, or is today

just an exception?" ask exactly what he/she has in mind.

> For example, "Did you want to see the research as well as the final recommendations? Was it all incomplete? Were there any parts that were acceptable?"

Asking clarification questions will buy you time to think of answers. It also causes the person questioning to either come up with real criticism or back down.

- Obviously, do the best you can. If you do not know something or have not brought something, admit it by saying how you will correct this problem. "I do not have that information. I will get it to you during the break." or "I will email this to everyone after the meeting."

- If you get a sense the person is hinting that you just do not understand because of an accent or language issue, recognize this as sabotage. Respond slowly and with an energetic voice, "Yes, I do have an accent, and I also know what I am talking about."

  They may ask where you are from. If it is not relevant to the topic or issue, respond with a smile and say, "I would be delighted to talk about my personal life after the meeting."

- After any of the above, you have the option to restate your idea or not.

The Interrupter

In a New Group/New People

- It is important to teach others how to treat you. People observe how you handle yourself in each challenging situation; most will use your behavior as a guideline of what is acceptable to you.

- When you want no interruptions, announce after your Opener that you would like people to hold questions until the end. In some companies, you can hold up your hand when interrupted and say "Please let me finish this." Call on the interrupter when you have finished your communication.

- When an interruption causes you to lose your line of thinking, review the last ideas and check your user-friendly notes.

The Interrupter You Already Know

- Greet the difficult person one-to-one when he/she arrives for the meeting with, "You always have good ideas. Today I want to present my ideas first and then take questions. I'd like to hear your ideas after I finish."

- After your Opener, state to the group that *you would like finish today without interruptions* and then take questions and comments. Since everyone hears this request, it is easier to ask the interrupter to hold questions.

  Say, "I want to answer your questions. Please let me finish and I will do that."

- Ask someone who handles those people well to mentor you on what to say and do.

People who have Side Conversations while you are Talking

- If your organization has always allowed people to hold side conversations during meetings, you probably will not be able to stop this distracting behavior.
- For colleagues in higher positions, decide if it would hurt your career to stop and interrupt them. Consult with trusted others about when and with whom you should stop this cross talk.
- People may be talking about your topic. They could be leaning over to say, "This is a great idea. Let's do it!"

Options:

- Make all the important points early in your talk before the interruptions and private conversations begin.
- *If you choose to interrupt them:*
  - Stop talking
  - Look expectantly at the talkers and ask,
    "Do you have a question?" or
    "Would you like me to clarify something?"
- This sets the tone that you will not accept others talking among themselves when you are speaking.

The "Know-It-Alls"

Thank them for their ideas! Be "impressed" with them. They want attention and want to look smart. They probably do this frequently to others, too. Instead of telling the person your idea, *ask* the person for advice or their opinion with, "Should we also take _____ into account?"

- If they take up too much of your designated time, interrupt with, "We certainly could go into that in depth. But first, I want to make a few other points" and go on. Make a valiant effort to finish your talk.

Snipers / Passive-Aggressive People

These people have very hostile personalities. In addition to using subtlety to attack peers and others, they often ingratiate themselves with superiors.

Snipers like to attack indirectly. They are quiet as they lean over and whisper to a colleague, "Sure, like he is going to follow up on this" and laugh. When you ask him to repeat what he just said, he will say, "Oh, nothing. We were just joking."

They try to hide their hostility by making it appear you are the one who has a problem.

- "You are too sensitive." or
- "You can't take a joke."

Do not attempt to make an equally smart or sarcastic response. Even if you win sometime, the sniper will return it endlessly since they have used this technique successfully since childhood.

Sometimes they will "play dumb" as if they can't understand what you say. Make them explain themselves. They must justify what was said or back down. You say,

- "I'm confused. I am no longer on that project. Why would you ask me about that?"
- "Please help me to understand why you want to know about..."

The first time you come across a sniper, you may get hooked into their game. You can prevent this happening again with preparation.

How to Prepare for a Sniper

De-sensitize yourself in rehearsal to the behavior and attacks:

- Ask a colleague to portray the sniper; the physical behavior, the tone of voice and choice of words. As you rehearse, have him interrupt with those behaviors that have made you defensive or made you lose your place. Have your friend suggest what to say and how to say it.

- After many times, you will still not like the subtle attacks but you will be in better control of yourself and how you react. Other workers will admire you for handling the sniper's behavior well.

Do not show anger at meetings regardless of the thoughts you have about this person. Don't become passive. Stay neutral and strong. You may never win the sniper over to your side but you will have the respect of others.

Difficult Groups, Difficult Situations

"What does it mean when they close their eyes and hold their hands over their ears during a talk?"

"They Only Listen for 5 minutes of my 15 minute talk!"

After five minutes, do the bosses begin speaking about your topic or go off on a different tangent? If so, give a five minute talk. If they should turn their attention back to you, explain your ideas further.

"They must attend a meeting and do not want to be there."

Open with, "You may be thinking..." and say what they may be thinking. (Do not say, "I know you are all thinking..." because the two or three who aren't may stop listening.) Then tell them why it is still valuable to hear what you will say.

For example:

> "You may be thinking, 'Why do we need another safety lecture when we have heard the same rules for the last four years?' There was a woman whose hair got caught in a machine because she was not wearing approved head gear. She is still recovering six months later and not able to work."

"I am speaking to clients disappointed by my company."

Open with, "We disappointed you. (tell what you had promised and what did not happen)."

Do not give excuses. Tell how you will correct all and do extra to hopefully win back their trust.

In the Body of the talk, use the Problem/Solution format to address each issue, stating the adjustments that have been made.

"I must deliver bad news."

Often, rumors have already spread about the difficult situation.

People are interested in how the bad news will impact their own survival. They want to hear that information as soon as possible. Therefore, get right to the point. They will not listen to any generic information you tell them before you reach the specifics affecting them. They will think, "Get to the part that impacts me."

- After an Opener, tell them about the situation and exactly how it will affect each of them. Tell them what you and the organization will do for them. Be complete and offer yourself as a resource after the meeting.
- Rehearse so that you sound sincere and concerned. People rarely forgive the speaker who delivers difficult information in an uncaring way.

You can Speak as Well as the Best Speaker You Have Ever Seen

About the Author, Reesa Woolf, PhD

Reesa Woolf, PhD, has mentored 3,000 corporate professionals to be excellent speakers. She is recognized as someone significant in bringing out her clients' best performance, permanently.

She has been honored as Senior Trainer in two significant C-Suite leadership organizations - the American Management Association and Drake, Beam, Morin, Executive Career Coaching. Her PhD in psychology contributes to lowering speaking & work stress.

Reesa was the Press Secretary for Jean King's Gubernatorial campaign in Hawaii. She was also an instructor at University of Maryland and Johns Hopkins University.

She has mentored individual executives, management and sales teams and delivered helpful, entertaining keynote speeches at conventions.

Reesa is known for presenting complex ideas simply and converting intimidating topics into non-threatening formats.

"Thank you" emails from clients in countless industries & technologies *report promotions, raises and more positive acknowledgement and more satisfying careers.*

Contact Reesa Woolf, PhD

(800) 769-6653

Outside the U.S. (973) 335-7361

info@ExecutiveSpeakingInAWeekend.com

WWW.EXECUTIVESPEAKINGINAWEEKEND.COM

WWW.FACEBOOK.COM/REESA.WOOLF

WWW.TWITTER.COM/REESAWOOLFPHD

WWW.LINKEDIN.COM/PROFILE/
VIEW?ID=16100450&TRK=TAB _ PRO

Participate in the Program - Executive Speaking in a Weekend

You will leave applying the skills that Confident Speakers use to Hold Everyone's Interest.

A pleasant and unique training experience that quickly teaches you how to engage and persuade, inspire and motivate. Available as *two-weekdays* or a *weekend*.

For executives, managers, sales professionals, business owners, and anyone who wants to speak like an executive.

Covers *every* aspect of *Writing* for each business situation included in this book and those you suggest.

Complete instruction on *Delivery* to use the skills professional speakers use.

- One-to-One Coaching
- Follow-up Critiqued Videos
- Follow-up Telephone and email consulting

Participant Feedback:

- A weekend of content and no-fluff.
- A weekend that is rapid-paced and fun.

- A weekend where you finally handle speaking issues and move ahead.

WWW.EXECUTIVESPEAKINGINAWEEKEND.COM/ATTEND-WEEKEND/

Provide a Speaking Seminar - for your Company or Convention

WWW.EXECUTIVESPEAKINGINAWEEKEND.COM/SEMINARCONVENTIONS/

Self-Study Program - Executive Speaking in a Weekend

Teach yourself how to Engage Listeners & Speak Confidently each day at work, and socially.

The Self-study Package includes:

- The *Executive Speaking in a Weekend Workbook* Immediate digital download
- Access to **live Executive Speaking in a Weekend *Teleseminars and Webinars***
- Discount to *Video-Critique* - Your video is critiqued with very specific suggestions
- **Bonus:** *Be Outstanding in Job Interviews* Immediate digital download

WWW.EXECUTIVESPEAKINGINAWEEKEND.COM/SELF-STUDY-PACKAGE/

Acknowledgements

Thank you

Mark Crandall, Lisa Berlin, Barbara Armstrong, Gail Tyrrell, Vasi Huntalas, Siobhan Wilcox, Dorrit Edwards, Adryenn Ashley, Jessie P. Woolf, Dr. Kevin Ross Emery, Tom Antion, Randy Glasbergen, Aisulu Gates, Stephen Edwards, Gerson and Ina, Francis Lamoste, Brendon Burchard, Isabelle Goldstein, Tom Quitt, Betty Lou Stambaugh, Pat Sanders, Herb Cooper-Levy, Pam Hendrickson and Mike Koenigs, Ida Sharagrodsky, Robin Pulverenti, Helen Street, Frankie Timmers, Arnie Hoffman, editors Kasi Rajan V, Suzy Beal and Joyce Jacobo and Rod Lengel.